Teachers Talking Tech

HARVARD EDUCATION LETTER
IMPACT SERIES

The *Harvard Education Letter* Impact Series offers an in-depth look at timely topics in education. Individual volumes explore current trends in research, practice, and policy. The series brings many voices into the conversation about issues in contemporary education and considers reforms from the perspective of—and on behalf of—educators in the field.

OTHER BOOKS IN THIS SERIES

I Used to Think . . . And Now I Think . . .
Edited by Richard F. Elmore

Inside School Turnarounds
Laura Pappano

Something in Common
Robert Rothman

From Data to Action
Edited by Milbrey McLaughlin
and Rebecca A. London

Fewer, Clearer, Higher
Robert Rothman

Teachers Talking Tech

*Creating Exceptional Classrooms
with Technology*

DAVE SALTMAN

Harvard Education Press
Cambridge, Massachusetts

HARVARD EDUCATION LETTER
IMPACT SERIES

Copyright © 2014 by the President and Fellows of Harvard College

Library of Congress Control Number 2014940442
Paperback ISBN 978-1-61250-746-0
Library Edition ISBN 978-1-61250-747-7

Published by Harvard Education Press,
an imprint of the Harvard Education Publishing Group

Harvard Education Press
8 Story Street
Cambridge, MA 02138

Cover Design: Ciano Design
Cover Photo: Getty Images/Comstock/Stockbyte/Getty Images
The typefaces used in this book are are ITC Berkeley Old Style,
ITC Legacy Sans, and Ruzicka Freehand LH

Contents

Introduction

THE NEWS COMES FAST, AND BREATHLESS, with each passing week: A major school district will spend tens of millions of dollars to buy computing devices for every schoolchild. A slew of teachers are using interactive smart boards to teach their students. Other teachers are asking students to watch short videos on the subject matter at home and to come prepared to work in the classroom on what would normally be considered homework. Still others are encouraging students to post to blogs, text each other, or create social media profiles for famous people. Some schools are allowing students to bring their own devices, such as smartphones, and even do work on them.

Meanwhile, it seems that every day brings a discussion about how much digital access students and teachers have to whatever Internet connection is available at school, and whether, in fact, that connection should be utilized to its fullest extent, or filtered, to protect students.

Finally, testing via computers—driven by discussions about, and adoption of, the Common Core State Standards Initiative (usually just called the Common Core) by most of the fifty U.S. states—is being discussed and implemented in many jurisdictions.

Even with tremendous awareness of technology and its potential impact on education, it can be difficult to sort through all of the relevant information, especially when it is set against other large issues in K–12 American education, which is itself going through a significant upheaval as a range of reforms have been introduced, addressing everything from pedagogy to school management. Still, a major piece of that discussion

1

has long involved debates about what technology ought to be utilized in teaching and learning, and in what kinds of ways it can actually produce improved learning outcomes. With public education budgets always tight, it has often been left to teachers themselves to figure out what technology to use in the classroom, and how best to use it.

In small but growing numbers, teachers are, in fact, figuring this out—in some cases with strong support from their schools and districts, in other cases, at least initially, just on their own. As the calls grow for integrating technology into the classroom in ever more impactful ways, it behooves us to look at what the teachers who are recognized in this regard—and for their teaching overall—are actually doing in the classroom. It would also be helpful to let those teachers tell the story of what they are doing. This is what I propose to do in this book.

With technology so woven into life, and with so many teachers developing, exploring, learning, and instructing, using some form of technology—from smart boards to smart pens—an examination of these teachers' experiences in adopting and integrating technology into their practices seems timely and needed.

Rather than a how-to-use technology book, of which there are many, or a laundry list of tech-based activities organized by discipline, device, or application, *Teachers Talking Tech* takes a reflective, holistic, biographical approach to explore how a range of award-winning teachers working at different grade levels, in different parts of the country, and in districts both large and small, have navigated the process of integrating technology in order to achieve particular learning goals for themselves and their students. The book profiles nine teachers who have become adept at using, manipulating, and evaluating technology, revealing their experiences, trials, methods, successes, failures, surprises, impressions, opinions, and analyses. A concluding chapter synthesizes their collective experience with incorporating new technology into their teaching practice—summarizing what worked well (and what less so) as well as what lessons can be drawn from their experiences. Finally, a brief appendix in tabular format displays demographic data for the nine school districts, including total enrollment and a breakdown of each district's student population in terms of race and ethnicity, percentage of special education and English Language Learner students, and eligibility for free or reduced lunch.

Unlike many books on the market now about ed tech, *Teachers Talking Tech* offers journalistic case studies of practicing teachers integrating technology into their classrooms, with a focus on their experiences and lessons learned. While many teachers blog about their experiences, no book has attempted to collect and distill their perspectives on the array of new tools that have recently become available. Therefore, this book will offer practicing teachers and pre-service teachers an accessible volume that condenses the wisdom of a range of tech-savvy teachers about how to think about, organize, and reflect on any new technological tool in the elementary, middle, and high school context. It should also appeal to school leaders, staff developers, and others concerned with technology integration in the classroom. Qualitative comparison and contrast of teacher experiences on the voyage of adopting technology would reflect many teachers' realities on the ground, which recipes, references, and policy analyses rarely address. Given the iterative nature of technology integration, and the fact that learning from mistakes is as useful as learning from success—if not more so—the book will draw out, chronicle, and synthesize a reality that is sometimes ignored in the current literature.

ADVANCING THEIR PEDAGOGY

Rather than using technology as an end in itself, these educators are using technology to advance their pedagogy. But what many other teachers want to know more about are the ways in which they are using technology—and perhaps as interesting, how they make the choices they make, and how they organize lessons that either relate to or use technology. In many cases, the technology provides some additional paths for learning, for interaction with the material, for assessing, and for covering more territory in a new, engaging, or different way.

It should be noted that the basic underlying pedagogy of these teachers includes all of the foundational pillars that one would expect of good teachers: solid introductions, scaffolding of materials, modeling, hooking their students' interest and engaging them in the material, varying instruction, and other such aspects. But in much the same way that someone with a kitchen outfitted with the latest gadgetry is not, de facto, a great chef, neither do these teachers rely upon technology to be superior teachers. Instead, they are superior teachers using technology to affect learning, and to amplify their underlying pedagogy and exceptional teaching skills. How they do this is the pith of the book.

In organizing each chapter, I found that many of the teachers organized their teaching, and their use of technology, around a number of tasks—some of them standard teaching tasks, like assessing, and some more in tune with Common Core standards, such as fostering collaboration and communication among and between students. Virtually all of these teachers value instructing their students in digital literacy skills. On this basis, the chapters are broken down into tasks that many teachers perform. They are largely the same, but they are not perfectly parallel for each chapter, depending upon that teacher's story, the particular grade level and subject focus, and the personal emphases relative to the students he or she is teaching. It should not be assumed, because a specific task is not broken out for one teacher as it is for many others, that this teacher does not focus upon that task—just that a discussion of the task in question is not as central to that chapter as it is to others.

Within the tasks, I tried to describe, and to let the teachers tell me, not just what they were doing, but how they were doing it, how they organized themselves to do it, and how they made certain choices about different kinds of technology—Web sites, videos, applications, and hardware.

One important task—fostering interaction with the content and material itself, rather than passive consumption of it—seems fairly ubiquitous within these classrooms, and so I chose not to break it out separately. It is suffused throughout the learning that goes on in these classrooms. Fostering interactivity can be smoother or more varied with technology, but many teachers have been helping students interact with the material for many years without it. One need only think of a reenacted scene from *Romeo and Juliet* in high school English class to understand this.

Many of these teachers, if not all of them, would reject the idea that they are spending time consciously integrating technology, as opposed to looking for more compelling, engaging, and efficient ways of delivering instruction and content. They see themselves as providing their students with the venues and platforms—along with the motivation—to interact with that content, and to become, in the words of one of the teachers, "uploaders, not downloaders," or in another's words, "producers, not just consumers."

This pedagogical perspective is supported and extended by the Common Core. And while I did not set out to restrict interviews to teachers who are working in states that have adopted the Common Core, all of these teachers do in fact work in adoptee states, and there is much in their discussion about their teaching that refers, directly and indirectly, to those standards, and especially to the four Cs: collaboration, communication, critical thinking, and creativity.

As noted above, one significant trend in this area is "interactivity," which seems to be a primary interest of these teachers when they do use technology. I describe interactivity in a very inelegant and nonacademic manner as requiring a response from students that is multiple in number, and iterative, and that potentially requires more complexity downstream in the response chain. Watching a video is passive, but creating a project like the one seen in the video, or generating questions to be researched and perhaps shared online with other students, from that video, is interactive.

As well, this book is less an analysis of these teachers' pedagogies, or of their use of technology, as it is a snapshot of what they were doing during 2013, from roughly February through December—that is, across parts of two school years. As such, I needed to let teachers tell me, and show me, what they were doing, and how they thought about what they were doing, as much as I needed to provide some biographical information about their lives, which would, in part, explain their instructional beliefs, styles, and practices.

By definition, this book provides only a glimpse of these teachers' practices, rather than encompassing their entire practice. It offers a look at some of the tasks they have been doing, in working more technology into their practice, and in a sampling of lessons. It is the result of many hours of phone conversations, e-mails, Skype calls, and also the sharing of Google documents, as I sought to improve the depth, reach, and ease of communication in which we were engaging. Teachers took much time out of their schedule to communicate with me, and to forward to me many artifacts of their careers, their teaching, and their students' learning.

I tended not to delve deeply into the areas that are external to teacher decision making. These are typically things like district grading policies (including items like minimum number of grades required per grading period), how platforms and learning management systems (LMS) are chosen, and their relative merits, and the choice of device operating systems and architecture (Apple vs. Android vs. Microsoft). That does not mean they do not hold opinions on these things, but rather that I thought I would focus on aspects of their practice around which they have significantly more say in, such as how to deploy the technology they have access to, which applications and Web sites they prefer (and why), and what drives the decisions they make to use, or not use, a particular kind of technology in a particular lesson, or series of lessons.

There has been a lot of discussion about purchasing technology for schools, and about the differences between school districts with large technology budgets and those without the available funds. Other than providing brief descriptions of technology acquisition and what these teachers actually have access to, my focus on the area of technology acquisition is limited. That does not mean, however, that this is a look at teachers with vast technology budgets. On the contrary, many have struggled to obtain the technology they are working with, and their acquisition and upgrade efforts have often been been slow and incremental. But one way or another they have acquired it, or at least enough of it to begin using it on a regular basis. These are not teachers with five unused, dusty old PCs at the back of the class, and the chalkboard and overhead projector at the front of the class.

In addition, all of these teachers have solid and widely available Internet connections, as well as a growing collection of hardware that in every case approximates, if not in actuality, a class set of devices. In some cases the devices go home with students; in others, they are meant for school only. In some cases, what is in class are desktops, and in other cases, carts of laptops. In some cases they are shared with another teacher or teachers. Also on display in some of these classrooms is student use of their own devices—often smartphones, but sometimes their own laptops or tablets. This phenomenon, widely known by its acronym BYOD (Bring Your Own Device), continues to grow in importance as teachers, including those profiled herein, become more comfortable with students looking up materials or accessing documents via largely mobile devices.

Another common feature is not often discussed, because devices and Internet connections steal so much of the public's attention, based upon media focus and district discussions. But, no less important than those two scene-stealers is having some form of virtual or network platform on which teachers can deploy a variety of materials to be shared with students, and where students can store materials they have completed. The cohort profiled in this book all control some form of accessible, virtual space for use in teaching. Not all of these platforms fit the description of an LMS, but they are used in ways that often approximate one.

With regard to assessment and grading of technology-based or infused lessons, I let teachers discuss this to the extent it was relevant, querying their practices in this regard only to the extent that it tied up loose ends for the reader.

It's a given that some kind of personal device—whether owned by the school or by the student—is likely to become a bigger part of a student's learning experience in the years to come, and that some amount of a given lesson will be experienced in digital format. But that is not the end of the story—it's the beginning. The teachers profiled in the chapters that follow talk freely about their experience of, and with, the technology that is becoming increasingly present in classrooms.

Educators reading this book may copy the uses, methods, and practices described by the subject teachers, or the reading may spark their own ideas about how to modify their practices to incorporate a new activity into their lesson plans that utilizes something—message boards, chat, camera phone, or any of a myriad of applications—to change their own teaching.

Teaching is changing, where it stood stock-still for many years. The rueful joke about the retired doctor entering a hospital after many years and finding it to be unrecognizable, while the retired teacher finds school to be utterly familiar, may soon lose some of its currency, if the practices of the teachers in this book spread further and wider.

1

"A Chance to Show What They Know"

Amber Kowatch

SECOND GRADE

Franklin Elementary School, Ludington, Michigan

Amber Kowatch is one of the very earliest elementary school Apple iPad adopters in Michigan. The iPad pilot in which Kowatch participated subsequently became the vanguard of a larger technology upgrade within the Ludington Area School District, after voters passed a $10 million bond issue to fund technology purchases and improvements. She later became a technology leader in her building, and then, starting in fall 2013, she began tackling technology coordination issues full-time for her region of the state. In 2012, she was named Teacher of the Year by the Michigan Association of Computer Users in Learning. Since then, Kowatch has also traveled and spoken often, in the United States and abroad, about her experience integrating the touch-screen tablets into her classroom, in a small-town county seat on the semirural Lake Michigan shoreline.

Kowatch exudes optimism about the devices and their software—the ubiquitous apps—and has pushed to use them more thoroughly both in the classroom and as an administrative tool. Her optimism stems from the greater flexibility, and fluidity, she believes the tablets have given her, including the flexibility to change many aspects of her teaching.

RAMPING UP

Like her young charges, Kowatch began small. She joined the faculty in 2009. Kowatch asked for a smart board first, and got it. As District Superintendent Andrea Large tells it: "When Amber came to us, she had had lots of tech in her old school, but we had very little tech integration in our building. And Amber came to me and asked for a Promethean board [a smart board brand] . . . We thought it would not only help student achievement but increase student engagement. We went to our parent group, and with them, we matched that out of our building budget."

Then, Kowatch was asked to be a part of a multiyear pilot by regional education authorities, in which every student in her classroom received an iPad. Once she started working with the iPads, she wanted to continue working with them, and in increasingly elaborate ways. As she became more adept at using this platform for lesson planning and instruction, Kowatch realized she could weave various aspects of the touch-screen tablet into her teaching, setting up something of a virtuous circle: as she used the tablet more, new opportunities for integrating the devices arose, according to her recollection.

She began placing more curriculum online, on a wiki-based teacher Web page overseen by the district, which she could edit easily, and which students could access on their devices.

This allowed her to start using the online platform as a combination class journal and storage—a sort of living syllabus—through the creation of a wiki. Wikis have been popular as free or low-cost catch-all Web-style pages for an organization—or a teacher. They serve as a home for lots of digital stuff: links, text, pictures, video, and more. Within that wiki, Kowatch placed a blog as well as links to classwork, assignments, and to apps the class used regularly. "My wiki became a large part of my instruction, as much as videos and books. I also learned that I could have my students create content and so could I," she recalled. Importantly, she could then display that wiki and its blog—and students could display their contributions to it—on the smart board, so that everyone in the classroom could see those contributions.

Initially, Kowatch was unclear how much she would actually use the iPads, or whether she would use all of the apps to which she had access (and could control access for students). She kept some of the apps turned off while she worked through the early phase of the pilot program.

"I installed a lot initially but I kept things off that were out of their reach," recalls Kowatch. "For example, none of my students were ready to explore multiplication and division the first weeks of school, so I didn't install apps that touched on those topics. I added the more difficult things later in the year to avoid confusion. Just like textbooks, we tend to start at chapter 1 and work our way through the book. It doesn't make sense to start at chapter 7 when chapter 3 is the foundation for that understanding."

"A little bit into my first year, I began to change my mind about how iPads should be used in the classroom. I knew from the beginning that I didn't want 'iPad time' written on my schedule, but I didn't know what that [full integration] should really look like with my instruction. Using just apps was not enough . . . I really started to push myself into using the iPads beyond app use," she adds—getting kids to take pictures, record sounds, and helping them see how they could get back to classwork or seatwork.

"I started out by just using the iPad for app-based lessons or activities. Before I knew it, I was using the iPad all the time, much beyond the apps. A basic example [is] in writing: I thought I would start by introducing the dictionary app. It seemed like a good tool for my students, especially my nonreaders. Students who have very little reading skills are not able to use a dictionary because they'll never be able to determine if they found the right word. They can, however, use a dictionary app that speaks the word once they think they've found the right one. In this way they are still using 'dictionary skills,' but they have affirmation once they arrive at the word," explains Kowatch.

"Once my students learned the writing process in my classroom, our writing time really developed around the iPad, and not because I planned for each lesson to be that way. My students were beginning to use all the resources they had access to on their iPad far beyond just the dictionary app. All of our vocabulary words, spelling words, content area words, etc. . . . became fair game for looking up. They utilized the topic lists we created at the beginning of the year, and added to our wiki to help get them started, and used many apps to publish their finished products. Even when I didn't intend for the iPad to be a part of our lesson, it always showed up inadvertently," she recalls.

As much time as Kowatch spends in front of students, and circulating among individual students and groups, she's also devoted a smaller amount of time to utilizing video. Flipping—the idea of doing homework during class time after students have watched a video lecture about the homework the previous evening—is gaining popularity in secondary school. For her primary school students, Kowatch performs a modified version of this, creating short videos that direct students, and sometimes substitutes, to perform a variety of tasks. "Sometimes it is to get them started and sometimes it is the actual lesson. It depends on the students' abilities and the actual lesson. Sometimes the lessons are to start the activity and sometimes they are meant to be more of a resource," she says.

She might ask students to seek out a particular lesson, in a particular place, on her class page, and ask them to pay particular attention to certain tasks in that lesson. That lesson might, itself, contain a video that shows students how to do something, or it might run them through the steps they need to tackle in completing the lesson.

Kowatch also began to create short videos of herself doing various tasks—for example, directing students to a particular lesson. She explains: "I did this for several reasons: If I had an advanced math group I would create assignments to get them started without me. Advanced students don't always need a teacher hovering over them, so I used that time to help my struggling kiddos, while they [advanced students] worked independently. I also created videos for students to watch when they needed additional practice. These videos could be used by parents as well. Another use is for whenever I'm out of the classroom. I can create lessons for the kids to do without the substitute having to know the ins and outs of the technology. This is especially helpful when I have a sub who isn't capable of, or isn't excited about, having all that technology in the classroom. The kids don't have to go without using technology, as I can give them the instructions through the video and the sub can just worry about managing the classroom behavior while the kids manage their own learning."

All of this took time outside of the classroom, but Kowatch indicates that she has also paid herself back, in time savings, by shifting to more online, immediate assessment, thereby reducing the burden of grading. With relatively more formative assessing, she says she better apprehends her students' learning progress.

Seeing that she could foster more independent and multi-modal learning for her kids, she began activating more of the apps, figuring out ways to use them more frequently—sometimes through experimentation. Among the factors she used in thinking about whether to activate an app were whether it would help introduce students to something for which they needed extensive practice. For example, mathematics apps related to multiplication and division were "out of reach" for her students until later in the year, when they were preparing for the relevant math unit. In other cases, she found that some apps—ones that contained a gamelike component in which students would "win" something, and the app acknowledged the "win," or right answer, with an audible shout or a visual award ribbon—were popular with students, giving them encouragement to tackle a lesson or to keep going with it.

Mary Jo DeMorrow, the district's technology director, who has been implementing much of the upgrade from the bond-issue money, says she and Kowatch are working to avoid the trap of "tra-digital" education—that is, traditional use of digital technology, such as electronic versions of existing, physical worksheets, that does not boost the level of interaction between students and the material beyond whatever interaction they would have had with the traditional format. Of some help to her integration efforts was the presence of technology consultants hired by the district to execute a larger, one-on-one deployment of the devices once the multiyear pilot wrapped up last year. She and other teachers were able to meet weekly with the consultants to review progress and discuss any issues that arose. She also attended a two-day summertime, consultant-run boot camp prior to mass deployment.

TEACHING DIGITAL LITERACY

Both Kowatch and DeMorrow recall the girl who was using her school-provided iPad at home when an error appeared on her screen. Remembering what she had learned about the device, the girl captured the screen with the error dialog as a picture, and e-mailed it to Kowatch to let her know something had gone wrong when she used the device. The next day, DeMorrow was able to walk through with the family of the girl a problem with the home wireless settings, which had caused the error. It would have taken much longer to figure out the problem, says Kowatch, had the girl not known what to do with the error on her screen.

For Kowatch, the girl's response was a small victory in developing digital literacy among her second graders. Notes Kowatch, "The language and skill set they learn inadvertently through using the iPad is amazing. My students know all about error messages, Internet filters, Wi-Fi, networks, etc. None of this was intended learning, but they have picked it up as a result."

One wonders how adept a seven-year-old can really be at doing schoolwork with a tablet device used by professionals worldwide. Kowatch answers that question by asking another one, which guides her literacy efforts: "How do we put this at their level?"

She expands upon this by noting that she teaches digital literacy "methodically" and "slowly," but ultimately, comprehensively. She adheres to a fairly rigorous, yet gradual approach to introducing the children to iPads, even as they are getting to know the classroom in which they will spend the next ten months.

"We keep them at school for one month, and take time to take ownership of the device. We'll plug it in, in the afternoon, and then it's ready for them to put on their desk in the morning. Then, it comes out in the morning and stays there," explains Kowatch.

Eventually, the devices go home with her students—and with them goes access to a large body of work, accessible for the students and their parents and guardians. Kowatch does show students how to type words on the device with the screen keyboard, how to snap a picture and embed that picture in a document, how to post a sentence to the class blog, how to use a drawing application to draw a letter or whole word, and how to annotate text from, say, a story they are reading. In short, they learn to pull content—a drawing, some text they have typed or scrawled, a video—into various applications so they can further manipulate that content.

Putting digital literacy at her students' respective levels means she also works with them on the basics of digital ethics and social intelligence, for which they have little or no background. For instance, she works with her kids to get them to comprehend that "they should never take a picture of someone unless they know they are being photographed. We try to set a procedure for that, so they will ask first," she says. "We have a lot of teachable moments when we're blogging, so if a student says [writes] something that could be taken in the wrong way, we have to stop and think about it."

This "thinking" expands upon how different kinds of media affect the consumers of that media. Kowatch works through the idea with students that when posting something online, we "can't necessarily hear each other's voices, and so we could take that remark in a lot of different ways. You might not know what the impact is. The world of Facebook will mean that they are typing things, and they don't realize the mark they are leaving."

"This comes into play when we begin to write letters. There are no LOLs," explains Kowatch, who emphasizes the formal nature of communication in these lessons. There are no "Hi Mrs. Kowatch" in the letters, either. "You begin an e-mail letter like any other: 'Dear Mrs. Kowatch,' and then you proceed and sign off at the bottom."

With all this, paper has not been exorcised from her classroom; she still uses some worksheets, and construction paper, and allows her kids a choice of tools to do certain kinds of activities, when they would prefer to engage in something more tactile than the tablet devices can provide, or when they just like the idea of using, say, crayon and paper. And writing often takes place in dedicated hard-copy "writer's notebooks." Overall, however, from Kowatch's vantage point, "what technology does for kids is allow them to communicate and collaborate" more effectively and more efficiently. She is facilitating these interchanges in many different ways.

MATCHING LEARNING GOALS AND TECHNOLOGY

Kowatch says that her decisions about how to use the iPad are formed by her and the district's aim to foster meta-cognitive skills, placing more of the responsibility for learning and for ownership of lesson content in the hands of students—even seven-year-old ones. One way to do this is to increase awareness of their learning.

Through the integration process, Kowatch learned that her students have a rudimentary understanding of meta-cognition. She also saw how engaged, and then motivated, they became when obtaining the kinds of instant, and in some cases automatically calibrated, feedback that an app can deliver for a right or wrong answer. Using these two bits of knowledge has driven some of her integration thinking.

She recounts a conversation: "I was talking with a technology rep the first year of my pilot, and I said, 'I need to better understand how they learn,' and he said, 'Have you asked them?' I threw up one question on a blog and I was shocked: they know who they are, and how they learn."

Learning styles were not a new idea for her; what was new was how aware her young students were of their own styles. Kowatch asked her students, "What ways do you learn best?," and offered them a range of choices. She got back a range of answers, including reading a book, listening to the teacher, talking, learning a song, drawing, and working with classmates, and some that were not on her list. "I was impressed that they would have thought about it, or even recognize it. There's no one saying it [the learning preferences] won't change; they are smarter than we think. I try never to say 'They're only seven.' Age is not a factor," she notes.

The idea is to get kids thinking both about how they learn, and how they will learn using the device—given that it can used for so many different things. In this way, it becomes a pathway to both learning and meta-cognition.

She introduces activities gradually. For instance, she describes how, as a "simple first-day-of-school lesson, I show sample graphs on my interactive whiteboard and students use Doodle Buddy [an app] as a whiteboard to display the answers [they write down] to the questions I ask them. The first day of school is all about first impressions, and I want the first impression with the iPads to be seamless, easy, and fun for the kids. I don't want to fuss with any of the messy stuff that technology sometimes brings about, so that is why I do this lesson first. All of the students get their iPads and come to the carpet at the front of the room."

"I put up some graphs," she continues, showing trends that involve numbers "about a store's sales of recreational equipment during week-days, on the interactive whiteboard, and ask students simple questions such as: 'How many red beach balls were sold on Monday? How many beach balls were bought on Tuesday and Wednesday?" etc. . . . The children write their answers on the Doodle Buddy app, which is essentially just a white screen with some basic editing choices like color, size, shapes, text, etc. . . . When given the prompt, they show their iPads so I can see the answers they've come up with. This activity replaces having to pass out chalkboards with dusty messy chalk and old socks or whiteboards with the markers that are missing caps or have pushed in tips due to overuse. I choose this lesson because it is simple and it 'can't go wrong.' This is key to making a good first impression. I can also use this lesson to start building some iPad etiquette with my students. I talk about how they should carry their iPad when walking around the room, how they should sit with it on the carpet, and how their iPad should be closed up until instructions have been given."

The success of this introductory phase has encouraged Kowatch to emphasize independent activities and to push more of the learning activity onto her students, by trying out an app or converting a paper activity to an online one. One favorite paper activity of teachers that encourages some independent learning is a scavenger hunt: to find a proper noun, to find something of a certain length or height, to find multiples of something. Students then draw that item, caption it, and it gets displayed or discussed.

In promoting independent use of the the devices, Kowatch has to find a way to also build both content and digital literacy skills. Scavenger hunts fit the bill, whether this involves finding proper nouns or items that are one meter long. In a previous incarnation, her students would have skittered about the room, or school, looking for objects to draw and then label on a piece of paper. These would then have been tacked up for display, and discussed. Later, students would take the drawings home.

Kowatch's new version centers on the device: students can use the devices to snap pictures of their target item and then embed it into a document—through the Macintosh Pages application or an application called My Story. They can then annotate the picture by labeling it or captioning it. One way is to show pictures—of vehicles like Ford trucks, New York City skyscrapers, and vegetables with names like carrots and onions—and then to help distinguish between general categories, like vehicles in general, and specific kinds of vehicles, and do this for each category. You might even ask a student to identify a proper noun at home, take a picture of it, and bring that work in the next day.

Next, they head out with a partner (or alone), taking pictures with the iPad of the objects they intend to use in the assignment; once they do that, they can then import that picture into the My Story app. They can also use the iPad's Pages feature to embed the picture, and then annotate it—labeling the item in the picture with the proper noun, or writing a very simple caption.

If students want to use the iPad to take a picture, on paper, of their proper noun, rather than snap a photo, they can do that, too. The reason this kind of physical participation counts just as much as the virtual content created by kids snapping pictures is that the student (or Kowatch) can snap a picture of that actual drawing and then upload it, whether to the class wiki, or to the student's online portfolio—or both.

FOSTERING COLLABORATION AND COMMUNICATION

Kowatch does not teach keyboard typing, but the students quickly learn to hunt and peck on the keyboard when they are not using an app that lets them draw out letters. In either case, they can annotate pictures or text with letters or whole words. It's helpful to have this flexibility when they work on vocabulary words, and when putting those words into sentences.

What Kowatch's class does with all these words they are learning— both from scavenger hunts and from vocabulary lists—diverges from traditional, nontechnology-infused classrooms in several ways. Students can access vocabulary words via a folder online, look up those words, and then write sentences—all on their iPads. They can then post those sentences to a blog or wiki where, during class, they can view their sentences along with other students' sentences.

"As soon as they answer the question or add text in some way to the blog, their answers will show up for everyone to see because it is a blog," says Kowatch.

As mentioned previously, students get to see the answers of other students, and those answers persist online as learning artifacts. For example, one lesson students access on their devices requires them to take vocabulary words, like "delivered" and "allowance," and use those words in sentences. Those sentences are posted within the blog, where they appear in a list of student submissions under the student's name. Students get to see their own submission alongside those of others—mistakes or no mistakes. Kowatch may discuss these sentences, but everyone gets to see a range of work from all of their classmates, amplifying the effect of sharing the work.

They can also annotate electronic versions of books—sometimes in PDF format, sometimes in other formats—and save those annotations, to refer to later or to share with other students, depending on how Kowatch structures the lesson. "We pull it up on a Doodle Buddy, circle the rhyming words, underline the similes," she explains. "Every week I plan and prepare for the next week. One thing I do is add on the new words. Parents know that words are added every Friday after school, so they can begin to prepare for the next week. Some families have more time on the weekends for spelling and vocab practice. The whole thing takes less than five minutes to add the eight to ten vocab words and fifteen spelling words each week."

DIFFERENTIATING

The changes to Kowatch's teaching have encompassed virtually all of her lesson planning, execution, and assessment. Two changes among many that come up whenever she speaks about the experience are the increased use of games and game-like learning software, and the ability to do more formative assessments, taking the pulse of learning in her room and adjusting her teaching to it.

The first of these changes addresses a big use of time in primary classrooms: how students practice basic skills—in math, in reading, in writing and word usage—in a way that targets the lesson to their skill level. Two kinds of software—self-adaptive learning apps, and games—are particularly appealing to Kowatch, given the hard work of practicing a skill that many students have never encountered before, or with which they have little experience. These two kinds of software are replacing in Kowatch's pedagogy a number of different paper worksheets.

Like many teachers, Kowatch has used paper worksheets—and still does, in select cases. But whereas in the past she found her students "hating" and "resenting" paper worksheets, she gets engagement and interest from students when they are doing the same problems in an iPad application like MobyMax, one of a number of self-adaptive programs. Self-adaptive programs are applications that, through complex algorithms, adjust the problem set that is displayed, in real time, as the student chooses correct or incorrect answers. So a student who chooses the wrong answer doesn't fail the problem set, but rather gets shown problems that respond to the particular issue that student is perceived to be facing, relative to the algorithm, as indicated by having chosen the wrong answer at that particular point in the sequence of problems. This kind of software is now used in curricula for reading, vocabulary, math, and other related subjects. It can be time-consuming to use, because a student who is struggling with the concepts being taught may be shown many more problems by the program, or work on many more examples, than a student who is choosing correct responses. But it differs significantly from the experience of filling out a paper worksheet, in providing real-time feedback to the student as the student progresses through the problem set.

"MobyMax is an amazing adaptive Web site," says Kowatch. "It works on all math skills and is tied to the Common Core. It also has vocabulary, reading, and writing components," she adds, noting that prior to the one-to-one program in her classroom (i.e., one computer for each student), "I don't know how I could ever have set up anything adaptive without some type of technology. We didn't have a computer lab or a laptop cart or anything in my building prior to the iPads in my classroom."

She likes these game-style apps, like MobyMax, because students stay engaged and interested in sticking with the lesson. Winning something, even a virtual ribbon or a computer-voiced "Yes!," remains interesting for children. "Two-digit addition with regrouping . . . it's a big skill for second graders. It's a lot of work for them to do problem after problem, and that's asking a lot of them," Kowatch notes. "But they will sit there all day and play a game that tests that skill. It gives them a blue ribbon and a shout. The motivation they obtain from it, because it's fun and engaging . . . it's the difference between working through a whole problem and not knowing how you did, and working the problem through an app and knowing immediately how you did. We spend all the back time, building the skill . . . They have to have a certain sense of a skill before they can even practice on a worksheet . . . 60 percent of your time learning the skill, 40 percent practicing the skill to master . . . at least of 20 percent of which is game-based."

Students in her class know where they are in a lesson, according to Kowatch, because the apps show them how they are doing and provide so much instant feedback. She guides this process, using manipulatives both real and virtual, along with cooperative learning in which students help each other.

Kowatch comments: "Before the iPad we spent lots of time focusing on hands-on practice. We use Unifix cubes to practice adding to the ones column and shifting them into the tens column once the ones column 'fills up.' Once we have our heads wrapped around that concept it is practice makes perfect. The kids do hours and hours of practice, practice, practice on worksheets during class time, for homework, and during small groups with me or the math intervention teacher. The students really need to repeat the skill again and again to master all the steps. Now that I have iPads, we still do the hands-on piece—it's critical for learning this concept. But the practice, practice, practice is a lot more fun for kids. There are countless apps that allow students to practice this skill in a fun way. It is much more motivating and exciting for kids and it provides immediate feedback."

"The practice . . . is mostly app-based. For this skill it is all about practice makes perfect. Rather than doing it on a worksheet, students can practice using an engaging app. The result is even better because it's timely, in the moment, and motivating. For this skill there is a lot of 'gaming' because it is complete skill mastery," she says, adding that some skills do need the "drill it and kill it" approach.

"Even though I hate it," she adds, "we still live in a world where kids need to have paper and pencil skills. I can't avoid that in the classroom. The idea is this . . . kids need both skills but will get significantly more practice out of an app than a worksheet because worksheets are boring and provide zero motivation unless there happens to be a child that loves getting a star on their paper the day after they've completed all that hard work. I can give a child a worksheet with twenty problems that takes them thirty minutes to work through, grade it that evening, return it the next day, find the time to remediate with them, give them another chance, and start the cycle back over or . . . I can provide them with a fun app and all of that will be accomplished in a much more timely fashion. The kids will have completed way more problems and get much better feedback like 'Great Job,' 'Way to Go,' flashing lights, cool sounds, and a real voice guiding them. Much better than just a star on an assignment from yesterday."

Differentiation is often a logistical challenge for many teachers. One way to differentiate has existed in classrooms for a long time. Learning centers, with independent lesson material that students tackle while the teacher is busy with other students, are common, especially in self-contained primary-grade classrooms, where students spend the whole day with one, or perhaps two, teachers. Kowatch blends the iPads with hard materials in most of these centers.

Kowatch sets up math centers online so that she can work with one tracked group at a time; the results of the students' work can be shown classwide, or remediated by Kowatch, as needed. To some extent this is no different from any teacher providing differentiated work, except that aspects of the logistical and administrative tasks normally undertaken by a teacher to provide that separate and more advanced work via a special set of materials, say, and then to collect it, are now handled by the student. Kowatch's young charges can find numbered folders online and access them. And they know how to save their work, to e-mail something to Kowatch, or to post it on her wiki or the class blog, if it's meant to be shared with classmates. Once kids working at a higher level are finished, that finished work can be displayed and discussed by the entire class, whether via the class blog, or on its wiki page.

Kowatch's students go to five centers—one for each day—within the classroom each week:

- *Listening/Library Center:* Kids can choose to either listen to a book on their devices or read a book of their choice—either on the device or as a hard copy. Throughout the day they are often told to read a book that is "at their reading level," so this center is a guaranteed time that they can use their free choice to read or listen to a story.
- *Book Report Center:* They complete a book report of their choice on a book from their reading tub. "There are many choices for this," says Kowatch. "I have a huge list of ways that they can complete a book report, but one of them requires using a book report app. The app e-mails the report right to me."
- *Writing Center:* Students have a weekly writing prompt that they must complete. Each week is different. "Sometimes they write a letter, sometimes they do a little research on a topic, sometimes it is a poem, etc."
- *Spelling Center:* At this center they practice their spelling words. "There are a couple of app choices for this, or there are binders with spelling activities in them."
- *Literacy Center:* "There are a few hands-on center ideas for this center that all revolve around reading or writing, and there are several app choices."

ASSESSING

A metamorphosis has occurred in how Kowatch assesses students. With her classroom technology, Kowatch also has the ability to create, administer, and share formative assessments more regularly—that includes sharing the results with her students, who she says are significantly motivated by the instant and informative feedback on their own progress.

She found that some outcomes have improved in a measurable way, using the tablet and its software. For instance, her class went from a measure of 62 percent reading proficiency in the year before iPads were piloted, to 79 percent of the class measuring as proficient in reading at the end of the following year—the first year she began using them. That speaks as much to the specific apps Kowatch deployed on the Apple tablet device, and how she incorporated them in lessons, as it does to the device itself. She saw early on that she could create quick, formative assessments—quizzes, check-ins for understanding—pretty easily, and then have students answer on their iPads, using student response apps like eClicker and Socrative.

"I definitely can do more formative assessment," she notes, "and then work in small groups" with those students that need more help. Students in her class are becoming enamored of the idea of throwing out questions for instant feedback via the eClicker app, whereby the students simply answer questions, and the results are instantly aggregated via computer. Afterwards, Kowatch's students get to visually see, in color, which questions a majority of students did well on, and which they did not.

Kowatch is particularly excited about how much formative assessment she can work into her day; she notes that it's not just useful for her to see more frequently how her students are doing and where there might be problems. It's also useful for her students, and it keeps them motivated. Instead of quiz and exam anxiety, she instantly computes the results from an assessment that they have taken on their iPads. Her system computes the percentage of students that chose the correct answer, and those are colored from green (most correct answers) to red (fewest).

While she works for kids who need more help, "my higher kids, I'll ask them to do a 'show what you know' project, or dive into that unit more deeply, and then showcase that for my lower group," says Kowatch. These higher-track "show what you know" activities are a blend of old and new technology; she also leaves it, in some cases, for the students to decide how they will demonstrate what they've learned.

For example, in math she might ask them to show what it means to multiply numbers. "Simple task with little guidance. I don't care how they show me, they just need to 'prove' that they know what this word means." For reading, "most kids would choose to record their voice and practice a passage over and over again until it sounds fluent. Great practice, whether I ever hear it or not, but even better when they get to demonstrate it to the rest of the class by playing their recording," she says. "Science: Show me what you know about the life cycle of a plant. Kids can create a book, a movie, an audio recording, pictures with captions."

Prior to iPads, "I never gave my students a chance to show what they knew. I wasn't that kind of teacher before iPads. Remember, I didn't know what my students knew until I got iPads in their hands. This is how much the iPad has changed me. My kiddos have opportunities they never had before," says Kowatch.

Kowatch also took the opportunity to put online the district's written six-times-per-year theme tests, which are used as district benchmark reading tests. Students go to a Web site via their iPad to access them, take them online, and the results are graded via computer, saving teachers, including Kowatch, "hours and hours." She shares those results with the students, breaking them down, and says, "It's very motivating for them."

She explains: "These are theme tests that are grade-level-wide at my school. These tests are developed by Storytown, which is a reading series our district uses grade K–2. The tests were created on paper, and I transferred them to an online storage warehouse that our district uses called Data Director," a Web-based assessment tool the district uses. "Data Director allows you to create assessments and administer them online. I give them to my students once every five weeks for a total of six throughout the year."

"This is a Web site my students use," she says. "Data Director aggregates and stores the data. It provides immediate feedback to my students and allows me to pull a variety of reports from overall scores and averages to specific analysis on individual questions. I tie the questions right to standards, and I always share this information with my students. I don't share names, but I do share averages and item analysis with the whole group. It's very motivating. It's a constant thing of knowing and seeing where they are . . . 'I'm getting it, I'm making progress,' or 'I'm not quite there.'"

NETWORKING AND PLANNING FOR THE FUTURE

Kowatch has given information, guidance, and support to other teachers, in an official capacity, and also seeks out ideas from others as she provides that support to fellow teachers. Guidance from technology administrators at the district and regional level has also provided her with ideas about changing her pedagogy to weave technology into the work of teaching and learning.

Another big source of support was the consulting firm hired by the district to manage the implementation of post-pilot deployment of one-on-one iPads; they offered regular training, along with visits by some of its professionals to see how technology integration was rolling out.

"The biggest change in my technology use has actually been the shift in my instruction. I used to stand at the front of my classroom and give information to my students all day long. Occasionally I would do a hands-on activity and have my students somehow demonstrate their understanding, but the core of my instruction was to just give information to my kids," says Kowatch.

She chalks up the ease with which her second graders have taken to the tablets to three factors: the ease of use, and the intuitive quality to many of the apps, facilitate her management of lessons and the students' ability to understand what they need to do; the fact that today's students are already exposed to many different kinds of technology, directly at home, or indirectly by watching what adults do; and the fact that once the initial introduction to the device has occurred, it, and the work created on it, becomes a "24/7 learning environment." As Kowatch observes: "It doesn't disappear."

"Kids naturally want to do well," she continues, "and somewhere along the way that can get squashed. Even those kids that are behavior problems—they do want to please others, but they don't know how. When you have an environment where we're always keeping tabs on them in a positive way, it's helpful too, we look at those colors [for the assessments] after every assignment. It's instant, everywhere. I don't share it by names, but it is powerful for them to see where they sit, to know 'Hey, I'm actually doing pretty well.' We're allowing them to control their learning behavior [so] they problem solve."

"I've yet to have a kid who didn't really get the iPad. I have had the kid who doesn't know what is right for them, with regard to what learning style they should pursue. For the kids who excel at using it, some of those kids will rise to the top, and be the leader, help the other kids."

"That's easier, because so much of the work of each student is available to the other students," she observes. As Kowatch sums it up: "It's changed my teaching in ways I never imagined."

2

Layering Technology
Throughout the Year

Pernille Ripp

FIFTH GRADE
West Middleton Elementary School, Verona, Wisconsin

Think you're smarter than a fifth grader? Perhaps, but you may not have communicated with as many people from around the world as the students in Pernille Ripp's class. At West Middleton Elementary School, in an upper-middle-class Madison suburb, Ripp uses technology to help her students connect with ideas, people, and places around the world. In 2010, inspired by a "passion for books" and hoping to generate curiosity in students about the "larger world," Ripp founded Global Read Aloud (GRA), a shared multiclassroom reading experience with an online component that allows teachers and students from different schools to communicate about a book being read simultaneously. It is a way for many classrooms to read the same book, usually read aloud by the teacher, and then use the Internet to interact about that book. The activities connected to the read-aloud are open to any teacher and class that wishes to participate. Since then, more than 140,000 students worldwide participate each year in reading the same book, chosen by Ripp from suggestions.

Ripp is also the author of the book Passionate Learners: Giving Our Classroom Back to Our Students *(Powerful Learning Press, 2013). Ripp's second book is scheduled for publication by Corwin Press in fall 2014. In 2013, she was nominated for a Bammy Award as Elementary School Teacher of the Year, and was called a Global Hero of Education that same year by Microsoft's* Daily Edventures *blog.*

IF YOU ARE IN Pernille Ripp's fifth-grade class, you are tweeting, learning how to search for legitimate, credible information on the Internet, blogging in ways that help students to develop posts understandable to students thousands of miles away, and combining various media to create coherent, cogent presentations. You may also be forming questions as much as developing answers, and providing your opinion about new technology recently tried out in class.

As she pushes her teaching and pedagogy to go above and beyond the content mandated by Wisconsin state educational standards, Ripp points out that she bears a special responsibility for preparing her students for middle school, where they head after leaving her classroom at school year's end. She maintains an attitude of constant inquiry and exploration, which she encourages in her students. Ripp is a fan of Twitter, and tweets about her work, presentations she is giving, or information and resources she has found.

Ripp asserts of her students' experience in the classroom, "We don't have any control over what they have to learn," because of state standards, "but we do have control over the way they learn it, by handing it back to them or by providing flexibility for them, and what they are creating, to learn the material."

RAMPING UP

Ripp pursues different strategies to educate her students about technology, while they all work to meet learning standards in their daily academic studies. An important one: she "layers" the technology, asking her students to use one piece of technology—say, Twitter—one day, or in one lesson, and then video, in another piece, until they have slowly broadened their knowledge of how to use a number of different technologies. The early pieces of technology that she teaches are reused in various lessons, so that students continually practice their use of these—like Twitter—while adding new tech skills to their quiver—like video or podcasting.

As noted, folding in technology—gradually, incrementally—is a theme of Ripp's teaching. Pretty soon, those steps add up to some real knowledge about how technology is used in academic work, and the students' level of comfort in using it, whether prompted or unprompted, is that much greater. And, like many a technology user and many an expert educator, Ripp has become comfortable with a high level of experimentation and frequent circumstantial adaptation. These characteristics have proven useful both in tailoring activities for her classes, and in providing venues for her students to produce new kinds of work.

Ripp's school district is affluent enough to have solved some of the technology integration issues that plague many other districts. Ripp has a smart board. She also has a set of four Chrome laptops, and the ability to check out others. BYOD (bring your own device) is not yet a reality, says Ripp. It helps that the district is small enough to be able to deploy "pervasive wireless," the Google Applications platform, and lots of devices, like video cameras. This infrastructure has allowed for a philosophy of technology use that synchronizes, broadly, with overarching Common Core values, such as encouraging meta-cognition among students—helping students to use the technology to think about their own thinking and learning processes. This can occur through evaluative exercises, such as reflections, or through other means, according to Ripp and her principal, Todd Macklem.

Among the educator stakeholders at West Middleton—Ripp, Macklem, other teachers, and the district's technology director, Jim Blodgett—there seems to be a consensus about using technology to push the boundaries of what teachers, and students, can do in a classroom, to boost critical and creative thinking. "We have the Chrome books, so they can research a lot of the stuff on the Internet. And then, to present it all, some of them have used Animoto, or Google Docs, collecting pictures and importing graphics into their presentation. Some kids are, instead, making a poster of their findings," Ripp observes. "It's neat to see what tools they are using, and what they are gravitating toward."

But just having access to technology is only the beginning of the journey for teachers, according to both Ripp and her principal. As Macklem notes, Ripp's teaching involves a large amount of reflection. He says that a big difference is that she's not afraid to record herself, or have the kids record her or her teaching. "She's willing to look at her craft, and with peers, not just with me; she's making the curriculum manageable, reproducible, re-purposeable."

Speaking of Global Read Aloud (GRA), he adds that its strength is in how many children it reaches and involves in learning at one time. "If it's something that only one child can interact with at a time, then I don't view it as very powerful. How can you make it something that is interactive for multiple children, or at least in which multiple children can reflect upon it—and with each other?" Macklem comments that Ripp is setting up her technology-infused lessons so that they are interactive, not just presentational. Discovery is a common activity: Ripp's students discover things—about their world, other people, and themselves. They might do that through research, but Ripp also explores communication among and between not just students but different classes as well, to foment cognitive connections. Among other things, Ripp does this by asking engaging questions, whether posting them online, providing them on a sheet of paper, putting them up on a smart board, or setting up stimulating hypothetical situations—encouraging her students to be creative in their responses.

An example of the layering strategy is GRA itself. She tries to make sure that she does all this, and for a fairly big project, early in the school year. Ripp comments: "My advice would be, to new teachers, to find a technology-infused larger project at the beginning of the year, to help students learn how to use the tech you have available to you. That way those methods can be used later in the year for other things, without you having to train students each time." Another big project is the assembling of a digital slide show examining the life of nineteenth-century African American orator and antislavery activist Frederick Douglass.

Like many teachers who want to challenge their students, Ripp begins any lesson in which students will work on a project by making sure she, and they, are asking the most engaging questions that can be developed, while still aligning the lesson with standards. In this case, that includes both Wisconsin standards and the Common Core State Standards. Ripp notes that not only does this promote higher-order thinking among her students, but it also ensures that she is folding digital literacy into as much of their work as possible.

For digital platforms, Ripp has used Kidblog and a wiki for student posting—along with Twitter, off of her teacher account—to connect her class to the wider world. She also likes a number of other tools for creating presentations, especially those that stream from the cloud—like Prezi. It means she doesn't have to worry as much about archiving the presentations, and students can refer back to them without having to carry around flash drives.

For GRA, different technologies are used. Some participating teachers use Edmodo, the Facebook-like social media platform for educators, to create groups where they can interact about GRA independent of students. Ripp also used Edmodo to connect her class with others, as well as Skype to connect to classrooms enabled with that video-call and conferencing tool.

Blodgett notes that "the idea is not to use tech just to use it, but to allow the students to see the processes they went through to learn what they are learning. That can come in the form of video diaries, or writing about their experience of a search, or of tweeting. From a philosophical and strategic standpoint, we recognize that we are not the provider of most of the tech that students are using, or will be using. So we're trying to build our system so that they don't have to use our technology to be learning."

MATCHING LEARNING GOALS AND TECHNOLOGY

Ripp talks about promoting authentic experience. By this she means creating situations in the classroom where students are learning not just about content but also about the ways in which they need to find, research, work with, and present the content about which they are learning—much as an adult professional would do in tackling a new project, utilizing new technology in the process. This comes up when students learn about how to use an activity called Mystery Skype. This is a game in which students from one class in a school might Skype with another class in a different school and try to guess where they are located by asking a series of carefully crafted questions. For example, explains Ripp, an authentic experience might involve "creating a video to explore how to do Mystery Skype better, because we are working on goals of presenting and giving instructions."

As Ripp sees it, "We never use tech to just use tech. It has to make sense as far as why we are using it. It has to fit with the goal. In science, for instance, they could use video cameras to create science diaries, showing me what they know, and what they are doing." Ripp might post this on the class blog or wiki, so that students "can then ask other science students or experts to comment and leave questions for them after they have viewed the video." The comments that are left might become a part of a future class lesson or discussion.

Promoting question-creation is a central aspect of Ripp's pedagogy. She likes blogging challenges, where students respond online to a question she has posted, and free-write a response. She often has a weekly blogging prompt, and provides time in class to respond. Perhaps the biggest difference between doing this in a paper journal and online is that the possibilities for sharing responses are greater using the blog. "I've posted one, for instance, that was pretty benign: 'If you could time travel, what time period would you travel to?' I did it just to get them blogging. And then, farther into the year, the questions get a little more open-ended; bigger questions, like 'How would you change the classroom?,' or 'Does homework help you learn?,'" explains Ripp.

She notes that at this age level, it can be a challenge to get kids to respond in great detail, unless the subject matter interests them. "You will see tons of kids blogging about sports, or something like that. To keep those kids, who are reluctant bloggers, interested, I might also ask them about their opinions. I get their opinion about how to start global education. A purpose is to get me to get their thoughts, so that I can change the way I teach. But it's also based upon their thoughts, so it also ties them into global discussion. It gets the kids thinking, too, about how they can change education."

She may not require blogging for every assignment. But one factor in encouraging students to do it, when it is not required, is to set aside some time. "I give them class time to reach out to other students on our blog roll [students in other classes] and to each other. I want the kids to naturally gravitate toward technology. So, I show them projects that they can do [with technology]," observes Ripp.

For example, during a science unit about landforms, "rather than have students do a worksheet, I gave them permission to film their experiments, explaining to me what they are doing and what is happening. They can then ask me to upload it to YouTube—blocked for students—and then we can embed it into their Kidblog. Sometimes I will open up our Twitter class account—password held by me—and ask students to live-tweet what we are exploring and send out questions for others to answer. Because all of the tools that have been used earlier in the year with GRA, I don't have to facilitate training but rather just let the students know of the option," she explains.

The landforms unit uses Full Option Science System (FOSS), which is "a research-based science curriculum for grades K–8 developed at the Lawrence Hall of Science, University of California at Berkeley. FOSS is also an ongoing research project dedicated to improving the learning and teaching of science," according to its Web site. Ripp did not choose the FOSS curriculum, and finds its technology tools "clunky," explaining that she prefers to use FOSS as a district-mandated framework, while finding technology—such as video—that she has already scaffolded and for which the students have procedures they can use quickly to show what they are learning.

For example, one of the social studies standards for fifth grade in Wisconsin requires learning about the special characteristics of U.S. regions—fossil fuel deposits in the West, for instance, or dairy products in swaths of the Midwest like Wisconsin, along with population and meteorological patterns in areas from Tornado Alley to the hurricane-prone Gulf of Mexico coast. Ripp felt that the standard, when taught as prescribed, would not be sufficiently engaging for students, and would not embolden them to do Internet research as deeply or thoroughly. She decided to add a layer of interest by asking them, via a role-play-inspired letter, to prepare for a "zombie apocalypse," and to analyze choices in small groups about where to go within each region that would lessen the chance of a zombie attack, while increasing the chances for survival.

As Ripp tells it, the letter to students begins, "'Dear Citizen, A zombie attack has taken place . . . ,' and students must decide where they will go, and how they will survive. In social studies, part of the Common Core is presentation, and [addresses Wisconsin] ELOs [essential learning outcomes] regarding land transportation, routes, and land regions. I thought about this, and to make it more interesting, how about, instead, citizens must survive a 'zombie apocalypse' and figure out which land regions to go to," recalls Ripp. "The zombies are coming . . . what will you do?"

"You know, students have to defend their choices," she adds. "I've really been a spectator, and it's been incredible to see the deeper conversations that come from it, and from their presentations, and their thoughts about it. This normally wouldn't really happen in social studies. I do have to figure out what I need to cover, but now the students are taking it in all these crazy directions, and having discussions that I would not have thought possible. As long as we know where we have to end up, there are a million ways to get there, so if a path we have gone down isn't working for us, then we change it."

Ultimately, after doing a variety of Internet research, each regional group presented their findings via Animoto, on a smart board presentation, which Ripp videotaped in order to show future classes and to use in her own professional development. In doing so, students were able to learn about Internet searches, assemble a multimedia presentation, use the smart board to present it, and learn to create and make a presentation with a group.

Ripp is mindful of the fact that project-based learning can overwhelm some students, and the self-regulation and pacing required to complete the necessary tasks can be too much for others. She recalls the situation of two students who were working together on Native American foodstuffs as part of a unit; they insisted they were making progress, but when they finally were required to turn over what they had done, they had little to show for their efforts. Because Ripp provides feedback, rather than grades, the students were allowed to write reflections about what went wrong, and how they could have changed the outcome.

FOSTERING DIGITAL LITERACY

For Ripp, digital literacy at the fifth-grade level often addresses standards that focus on using the Internet to evaluate information and its sources for qualities such as integrity, independence, and veracity.

"They [the students] will ask, 'How do I know it's a trustworthy source?' Well, we have to evaluate it, and we need to credit sources. You've got to say where you get this stuff from, even when it's on the Web," says Ripp. "Sometimes I do just say, 'You need info on this.' They can get so overwhelmed that they don't know what to search for. So then I realize we need to have a lesson on this. It's awful for the kids, too, to just kind of go on the Internet. That's why we use Sweetsearch"—a curated Internet search tool geared to K–12 students—"and we have filters."

"Crediting sources—that's really part of fifth-grade standards," adds Ripp, who tries to push beyond the standard to help students critically evaluate what they find online. "They need to use resources from the Internet—that's another one. Well, that's kind of blah. What's blah is just the standard of using the Internet to search for stuff."

They also need to know about evaluation, and they need to have some digital literacy for when they go to middle school the following year. Ripp senses the standard for Internet usage at the fifth-grade level does not really encompass enough discernment skills that would enable her students to evaluate the quality of sources. For her, some of the tech-heavy components of her pedagogy—such as GRA and Mystery Skype—are just two of many examples that perform double duty as ways to help students do more than a technology-based task, by both interacting with the material as well as learning computer and digital literacy skills.

She likes shareable document platforms like Google Docs, because they create a digital "paper trail" for the entire year. And she likes the sharing capabilities, and being able to jump in and out of documents. Ripp will take a look at one of her students' first drafts, and if some student input seems amiss, or headed in the wrong direction, "I'll say, 'You have to work on this,'" and leave that as a comment. That comment can be accessed by the student, over and over again, as they work on the document.

Anything that will provide a window for her kids into the larger world, and from which they can examine more sophisticated content and materials in a safe and secure way, appeals to Ripp. They have to be able to respond to hypothetical questions, as part of the standards. And Ripp wants to see them become comfortable with blogging, and with responding to other students' blog posts. So she starts out small.

For Ripp, the technology is not the issue; what is important to her is what questions are posed using it, and how far she can push its use to exercise her students' minds in service of those "blah" standards. In order to digitally archive and collate multiple sources, Ripp sometimes uses a Web site application call LiveBinders. "If I am giving students specific sources I use Livebinders, and collect a lot [of different sources for students]. I will then have a student log in or use one of their logins to see if the sites work. If the students are researching broader things, which is what we do most of the time, then they keep looking for sources that are not blocked, or they put down specific sites to access from home. In a pinch I will access to get information for them. We have worked on different ways to organize our research such as notebooks, notecards, Google Docs, etc. They tend to use Easybib for their sources."

She describes lessons on searching as "organic" and varying from year to year, depending upon what else they have covered and how far along the class is in the curriculum. She's fond of a popular spoof Web site that lays bare the hazards of accepting the Internet as gospel. For example, "Last time we did it, I had a handout we use to see whether a Web site is a good Web site or not. Then I directed them to the Flying Octopus Web site and had them evaluate the site using the sheet; this way it led into a conversation of how even fancy Web sites may be 'bad.' I usually just show them shortcuts on how to search Google better, and also just how to use Sweetsearch.com, which is a curated, student-focused search engine. I really want students to leave fifth grade with various ways of doing research as well as a sense of knowing what works best for them. We have so much information out there. We talk about student choice, and voice, and giving them tech; they also need to have the skills to make choices" on the Internet, asserts Ripp.

FOSTERING COLLABORATION AND COMMUNICATION

Global Read Aloud, the project Ripp started in 2010, is a way for students in different classes to be read aloud to, and then connect about the book with other students doing the same thing. This can occur at any point during the actual read-aloud—before, while they are being read to, and afterward. And the "connection" can occur via any number of online tools, such as Skype, Twitter, or blogs. Ripp is its organizing figure, around which the read-aloud coalesces, but she has sought to avoid rigidly managing the experience of the activity. It's up to the participating teachers to figure out how they want to connect with other classes, and what they want to do with that connection. Some classes have Skyped with each other, to give their opinions about the book and to hear other students, whom they do not know, opine on the same book. Some classes, like Ripp's, have made or posted predictions about what they think will happen. The actual reading aloud of the book in Ripp's class takes place as it would in any other class; however, there's an emphasis on connecting through the Internet with other classes reading the same book that allows her students to communicate with other classes about the book in various ways.

Ripp comments that participating teachers in other classrooms "just have to read the designated chapters within the week and then finish the book, preferably within the time frame. Some don't, and that is fine, too," she says, adding that "most activities take place after we have read aloud . . . but I have done live read-alouds as well," in which she reads aloud while both her class and another class listen via the Internet.

In Ripp's words, "I use the Global Read Aloud to add layers of tech, so that through the project I introduce one thing at a time, and show the kids how it is used, and for what specific purpose, by us. It's very simple: I read aloud every day, and then we discuss. We have a couple of classrooms; we are connecting with them, and we might go on our Edmodo group" to post something, like a presentation, video, or a link to the wiki or blog posts. "And we might be creating something more global, like creating something on Edmodo, and then tweeting that out, and then putting that on our blog. In taking our book and reading it aloud, and sharing that, we just amplify that, and invite other classes into our intimate circle."

Prior to the Global Read Aloud, which takes place in mid-fall, she will suggest several books on her Global Read Aloud Web page. Once the book is chosen, Ripp leaves it up to the teachers who have signed up as to what they do to connect with her, or with other teachers. "It's so vital to the rest of the year, as this is their first foray into putting their voices out there," comments Ripp.

Ripp now spends time planning GRA, but like social technology it-self, GRA seems to have grown very much in an organic and unplanned fashion, as more and more teachers have become interested in partic-ipating. It's a lesson writ large, that grew to include many classrooms. And Ripp has taken each cycle as a way to expand her class's technology footprint and to explore how she can connect the read-aloud with more classes—but also have more teachers connect with each other.

Initially, Ripp chose to read *The Little Prince* to her class. She then tweeted about it, and caught the attention of some other teachers. Ripp then created a blog for the book reading on Kidsblog. The class spent several weeks on the book, and then she encouraged her students to blog about the book via Kidsblog, a secure way of blogging. Her stu-dents wrote about themes they found in the book, and they then re-ceived comments on those posts from students in other parts of the globe, Ripp says, while promoting their participation with a hashtag that Ripp created with her class account.

GRA is also a chance to practice the blogging that she has been working on with her students since the beginning of the year. At the year's start, "we take two to three weeks; we do paper blogs, and we tear apart my blog, other classes' blogs. We discuss what the purpose of a discussion online is. I am the only one who has the Twitter account. They can practice with Twitter; they can do journal entries. They learn how to create an ongoing conversation through examples and model-ing. Some of them can see how a good post can get comments. They'll say, 'I got eight comments on this one.' And I'll ask them what they have learned from that kind of success. Others will say, 'I haven't gotten any comments on this blog post.' To them, this is an awesome tool. [Stu-dents will say,] 'I'm going to do this and this, and get lots of comments.' And they will do crazy fonts, or their friends will call them out and say, 'We can't read your post,'" says Ripp.

But, notes Ripp, "The blogging is so much bigger than that; it's about the global connection with others, and setting up a connection with other classes—otherwise it's just word processing. We were blog friends with a class in Egypt, and then the Arab Spring occurred. Those [Egyptian] students, they go to pyramids for field trips, and they had a front row seat to what's happening in their country."

Once students had blogging down, Ripp guided them in creating short videos about the book, including drawings her students did, using a common online tool, Animoto. When she found that her students were farther ahead of some of the other classes reading the book, she asked them to tailor their blog posts so as not to provide plot-spoilers. Ultimately, she wrote, her kids appreciated the activity using technology because they now had a way not just of connecting to others, but also "of bringing the world in."

Ripp is a huge proponent of putting student work online, and of students sharing their work and presenting that work online. But she has limits, and if there is a "failure" in getting a project completed, "you want to be real careful about putting a failure online." Project-based learning, when using technology, involves multiple steps, and it does not always work out. And with all the choice and information out there, "kids need processes and guidance."

Sometimes things are a little easier. Many of her students were excited about the idea of communicating with the class in Egypt as the Arab Spring events unfolded. And they were equally thrilled to communicate with children's book authors Katherine Applegate, Tom Angleberger, and Neil Gaiman. For Ripp, this was not terribly difficult to organize. She created a classroom account on Twitter so that all of the inbound, and outbound, communication funneled into one place. Her students could then always find the information imparted to them in that one account, eliminating concerns about her students' security.

Twitter is a great vehicle, Ripp believes, for helping students to connect to the wider world in a prescribed way that offers some narrow parameters. At this juncture, in their digital odyssey, it is more important that they see the possibilities and learn to present ideas effectively in a succinct manner; more complicated projects, in which huge amounts of information and data have to be exchanged, come later. It is engaging for students to be able to communicate with people outside of the classroom, who may not be able to speak to that class face-to-face, she says.

REFLECTING

For Ripp, technology use is more than a cycle of teaching, use, and assessment. It's also an ongoing "conversation" in which a "toolbox" of technology tools that the students own, and can use, continues to grow throughout the year. Moreover, Ripp seeks out her students' impressions of the technology that is used, whether it is a Web site, application, or device. She does this for nontechnological issues in her classroom, as well.

"So much of my teaching is dependent on the feedback I get," comments Ripp. "I have changed how we function as a classroom such as seating, rules and expectations, and various procedural items. More importantly, I have changed how I teach and deliver content in many topics. Very little 'sit and get' goes on in the room, and I have used the feedback to circle back and redo things. We have also used the feedback to work on community and other deep-feeling issues in the classroom that I may have missed in the day-to-day."

She adds, "I think that because students know I will listen to their suggestions and feedback, that they become more honest in it. They try to tell me what isn't working, but then also offer up solutions. We have so much information out there, we talk about student choice, and voice, and giving them tech. They need to have the skills to make those choices."

3

Interweaving Technology and Art

Jennifer Motter

SEVENTH TO NINTH GRADE
ART
Forest Hills Middle School, Sidman, Pennsylvania

Visual arts programs are more often the target of budget cuts than the focus of technology upgrades. But, well away from much-galleried and museum-heavy cities, in a rural area near Johnstown, Pennsylvania, Jennifer Motter is leveraging support from school and district administrators and teachers to remake her school's visual arts program, spanning grades seven to nine, using technology as part of a transition to a new state-of-the-art middle school/high school campus to open in 2015.

Just two years ago, Jennifer Motter obtained her PhD in art education from Pennsylvania State University (PSU), publishing her dissertation, "Feminist Art Curriculum: Politicizing the Personal via Cyberpost Activism." At Forest Hills Middle School (FHMS), she's blazing similarly progressive paths for students, the school, and the school district, by incorporating technology into art instruction. One series of student projects—guided online research and art-making explorations called Web quests, developed in collaboration with her alma mater—made local media coverage and earned the admiration of administrators.

Motter has also instructed at a PSU-affiliated Tech Savvy Camp for middle school girls, worked as a digital graphic artist during breaks, and recently obtained her K–12 state technology certification. At art education conferences around the United States, she presents with other educators about technology-forward visual arts education. Influenced by her own high school art teacher, and her PSU doctoral adviser, Motter says that she's driven by her love of "digital art-making." She, and the district, share a belief that art-related careers are something students need to have access to, whether as graphic designers, animators, or filmmakers. Because of this, Motter says she is determined to use her art classes to "help students attain knowledge and skills that will prepare them for the twenty-first-century workforce and higher education."

RAMPING UP

Motter's hiring has been both the reason for, and the impetus behind, upgrades to technology used for the visual arts at Forest Hills. District and school authorities were already interested in growing a technology-infused art program at Forest Hills. Motter fit the bill. Although the Internet connection was reliable, various corners of the Internet were roped off, to protect students from adult content and to forestall issues like cyberbullying. In her first year, Motter spent considerable time addressing these obstacles.

So the going at FHMS was a little rough at first. She had some, but not most of what she wanted in the way of tech hardware. For someone who was planning on using a Web site like YouTube to expose students to artists and to post some projects, there have been a range of obstacles to overcome—from filters that prevent students from accessing the site entirely, to issues of what she could post and how she could post it. These included some student work, as well as posts of videos of artists at work. However, utilizing the advice and help of a teacher mentor, planning for the future, and showing the work of her students to school administrators and the community, Motter has gained the trust of the school, and is continuing to expand her curriculum and its use of technology.

One of the first indications that Motter's school was open to change came in her assignment of a mentor who was not, strictly speaking, in her discipline. Motter's mentor, technology department chairperson Kevin Lang, who teaches problem solving and computer-aided drafting, is a long-time FHMS teacher.

"Dr. Motter came to Forest Hills with very good time management skills and organizational skills; as her mentor, I did not have to help too much in these areas," recalls Lang. "Basically, when Dr. Motter would come to me with ideas for projects, she would have the outline of what she wanted to accomplish already in place. My only suggestion to her was to allow extra time in her preparation for the unforeseen that could happen when integrating new technology."

So Lang, together with Forest Hills administrators, helped Motter find the technology to begin remaking the curriculum, and then implementing it. Motter recalls that she was able to begin working on her plans quickly because of the existence of a computer lab that she could use several times a day when it was not in use by another class. Meanwhile, in her classroom, Motter had some desktop computers; late last school year she was also able to obtain a small complement of iPads and a Mac Book Pro. In addition, the computer lab in her wing of the building received new computers in the last two years; these new computers are loaded with the Adobe design software Web Premium Creative Suite 6—"installed for my use," Motter says.

Some of her struggles have involved YouTube access, which is critical for allowing her to model the work of other artists for students, and for her to post student work in which video is used. The Web site is also used to model the progression of steps for an assignment: for example, to show the steps on a Web quest, and for recording and presenting student-created stop-motion animations—projects she meant to undertake as part of the new curriculum taught later in her first year.

Motter also wanted to use YouTube to post some of her students' video presentations, although she promised to monitor comments and adjust privacy settings to protect student identities. Initially, the school nixed that idea, and Motter ended up posting on her district homepage.

The first year progressed in fits and starts. "I requested a class set of Mac Books for my students through a special budget for this school year. However, this request was denied, as I was told that I will receive these computers when a new middle–high school is built in two years." Recalls Motter, "Being a new teacher, I seemed to be less trusted and had less authority than experienced teachers. But I was also requesting permission to do what hadn't been previously done at my school district."

Gradually, the YouTube situation resolved itself, as Lang and others jumped in to address it. "After this original request, a school district YouTube account was created by teachers of a problem solving [gifted technology] class," recalls Motter. "Alternatively, I posted the stop-motion animations at my FH [district-based Web site run off its own servers] blog, as the video file size was small enough. The following semester, my tech ed mentor and a gifted teacher who teaches a problem solving class were permitted to create an FH YouTube account to post a video for a contest. After asking if I could also use this account during my second semester at the district, I was allowed. I used it to post antidiscrimination videos produced during a Web quest."

A big plus for Motter is that her teacher Web site, where her FHMS blog is located, is flexible enough so that she can use it to post everything from assignments, to student work, to digital resources—such as royalty-free picture galleries and technology-use tips. "Every teacher here has control over their own teacher pages, and she's done blogs, and she's done picture galleries; teachers can get comments on the blogs and respond back," says Lang.

Still, Motter had Lang, and the larger vision of a technology-friendly school—if not in this building, then in the new one—on her side. With this in mind, she developed a multiyear plan to acquire and integrate the hardware and software needed to accomplish her curriculum development goals. "She came into a traditional art program, with a very good studio art classroom," adds Lang. "I was interested in looking at different printers, computers, and software, and led her in the right direction to acquire those. She wanted to buy some digital cameras, and we had a budget for her so she could order some stuff, and hit the ground running. We also had some older computers being refurbished with more memory; we had that done, and I just helped her with her vision."

Motter is methodical in her planning, offers Lang. "She has created a scope of sequence on where she sees her curriculum developing in the future and what technology she would need to accomplish her goals in the curriculum. Dr. Motter has utilized the district's special budget process to gradually obtain new technology for her developed courses. Example: This school year she requested a new color laser printer, an upgraded LCD projector with the capability to utilize an Apple TV, upgrade Adobe software; she has also received a teacher iPad and one MacBook Pro laptop computer. Next year she has requested six additional MacBook Pro laptops. She is in the second year of a three-year plan to build the technology to a point that it will meet the needs of her curriculum; the goal is to have enough Mac Book laptops to sustain an entire class once we move into the new building," Lang wrote to me.

MATCHING LEARNING GOALS AND TECHNOLOGY

Motter talks about "interweaving" technology and art. "I use the term 'interweaving' to represent a smooth, continuous blending of technology into curricula that I strive to maintain," she explains, adding that "continuous, routine interweaving of technology into art curricula is more effective than randomly integrating technology throughout the school year."

As a new teacher, Motter developed a number of technology-based activities and lessons that expose students to the wider world of "art making," cultural issues related to art, and digital presentation skills that they will need in their future school and work careers. Among the activities they worked on were a Web quest that served as an online cyber-exploration, and then other activities, such as a digital storytell-ing, and stop-motion animation. As part of this, she developed activities that also scaffolded the use of the hardware itself, such as iPads.

For many of these assignments—which involve multiple steps, mul-tiple pieces of technology, and art making—Motter explains that her planning process involves managing a timeline and breaking pieces of the curricular unit down into chunks. "I keep a calendar. I have to write things down. I break up project procedures into steps while writing unit plans prior to implementation," she told me.

Early in the year, Motter incorporates—and has insisted that her PSU collaborators incorporate—time into technology-based lessons for learning how, say, a digital video camera works. Usually, that learning about hardware precedes learning how the software will take the output of a video camera. It's a piece of the puzzle her students need to know about. This was especially true for the stop-motion animation unit that grabbed administrators' attention about the possibilities of Motter's cur-ricula, and generated excitement about it within the district. Once stu-dents were apprised of how to operate the video cameras, they followed YouTube-based tutorials about how to import hundreds of digital still pictures of their stop-motion animation subjects into editing software—in this case, Movie Maker.

"The stop-motion animation assignment was highly successful, as it captured students' interest and motivated them to engage in art mak-ing," recalls Motter. "Dr. Keifer-Boyd [dissertation advisor and art edu-cation professor leading her PSU collaborators] and I were particularly impressed with one of the stop-motion animations," she said. "We were particularly impressed by the technical ability and creativity that one of the stop-motion animations demonstrated. This video was intricate, including smooth movement and transitions, thoughtful in design, and well planned and executed. It also sent the following meaningful mes-sage to the viewer: 'Let your imagination run free.'"

"My principal viewed this animation and shared it with the superin-tendent," she went on, "who shared it with the school board president.

The first semester, I e-mailed Dr. Keifer-Boyd the stop-motion animations [to post online]. The second semester, after a district YouTube account was created, I posted the animations online. I edited the privacy settings for monitored comments, to prevent spam and outside comments."

Given that much of what she's presenting is new to students, she looks for a way to "hook" students initially, so that as they move into learning about the project they will work on, the students "support" the project idea. By "support," Motter says she means students take an active and enthusiastic interest in the project, rather than just ticking off the many tasks that are involved in executing it. For example, one Web quest asked students to curate a themed contemporary art exhibit; Motter used a video to introduce students to, and motivate them to work on, the Web quest. "I use a hook—like a YouTube video—to help motivate student interest and participation," she explains.

For the Web quests, she collaborated with PSU undergraduates who supplied the content for them based on Skype discussions between herself and the undergraduates. For other lessons, Motter typically develops ideas "on my own, or tweak projects that I've seen in art publications or art shows, or that I have done before myself. I then do some research to find references, such as Web sites and YouTube clips, to show to students to support my project idea, capture students' interest, connect what we are doing in class to the contemporary art world."

She also covers elements of art, principles of design, and postmodern art principles in her lessons, using—and teaching how to use—Photoshop and various Web sites, including the Digication initiative, sponsored by the National Art Education Association (NAEA). Motter says, "I teach students how to use different tools and application functions, as well. I use a scaffolding approach as I teach simple digital imaging techniques, and then move to more advanced concepts, and tool usage with each Photoshop project."

To organize a unit on digital storytelling requires modeling a variety of technologies that allow for capturing, creating, and combining audio, video, and text. Motter provides a lot of downloadable instructions on her district Web site, and works through the technology issues in class. But she also has to instruct students in what storytelling means within the context of the digital and visual spaces that are integral to the class curriculum and content. Resources explaining in detail what storytelling is can also be found on her Web site, so that students can read up on this and use a variety of links to help them understand the concept further.

Other important pieces of Motter's assessment regime: she has her students use rubrics to assess their art projects, along with the class blogs to comment on others', and their own, projects. Motter scans the blogs to record initials and class periods for the "artist's statement of reflection"—this is writing online that her students do about their own work and students' online critiques. "Throughout the semester, I ask all students to participate in peer critique by posting comments on artworks for which they have feedback," Motter explains.

FOSTERING COLLABORATION AND COMMUNICATION

One of the most successful pieces of pedagogy has been the Web quest, which Motter has adapted for use in her curriculum. When first conceived of, at the dawn of the Worldwide Web in the 1990s, Web quests were something like online treasure hunts; now they are being used to help students explore and assimilate different kinds of content in an interactive way.

In Motter's case, they are online exploratory research projects, developed by university students specifically for her classes. Through these they create art related to the Web quest topic. These Web quests seek to explore contemporary issues, art, or artists, in a way that culminates in a student work that can be shared, physically and online, and could then be the focus of feedback both from the university students and from Motter's own students.

Motter comments, "Much of contemporary art focuses on local and global issues. So the Web quests are issue-based and expose students to contemporary art and art-making practices. Through the Web quests, and my other project assignments, students are able to relate to contemporary artists, when they [the students] are challenged to explore similar themes and techniques."

The initial development of the Web quest curriculum brought together pre-service art educators at PSU—students themselves working toward K–12 teaching credentials in art education—with Motter's classroom. Motter mediated the process with the university class, which was titled Art Education: Visual Culture and Education. She could have developed these on her own. However, in an example of synergy between high school and higher education, Motter and the art education class at PSU developed the projects for her classes, and then provided feedback on the middle school students' work, helping the middle school students obtain outside perspectives, and these in turn helped students to think about their own work and to develop new questions about it.

The two schools—Forest Hills Middle School and PSU—are nearly eighty miles apart, virtually prohibiting repeated meetings with the art education class. Motter, therefore, Skyped with the art education class, answering their questions about the focus of the Web quests and the criteria upon which they based their Web quest development, including such items as the student population, school district, technology access, students' prior art- and technology-related experiences, and course and student learning objectives. After these Skype meetings, the university students proposed various quests and posted them on their PSU course blog to await Motter's feedback. Once that feedback was incorporated, PSU students created a series of fully developed Web quests for Motter to use.

Initially, the PSU students developed Web quests for grades seven and nine, providing a total of seven quests, one for each period Motter taught that year (she had three preps, one for each grade). Among them were thematic searches and activities that focused on a particular subject matter, such as street art. Last year, this was expanded to include grade eight. Given the somewhat more conservative milieu in which Motter was teaching, "I was cautious of Penn State students' terminology in

Web quests. I requested that Penn State students define terms that could be misinterpreted, such as 'feminism.'"

In one quest, "Urban Expressionism," students learn about, and ultimately create, street-style art, à la the British iconoclast and street artist Banksy, as well as a number of others. The PSU students introduce the topic by presenting a digital map that preloads the locations—and links to actual photographs of the art—of street art from around the world, in Asia, Africa, South America, North America, and Europe. Lang, Motter's mentor, calls the Web quest project "a good example of utilizing time management skills with the integration of technology. The collaboration project allows the college students to try out their activities [Web quests] in a real-world situation with actual [middle] school students. This allowed for continuous feedback and modifications to be made as the activity took place."

Each Web quest ranged over very different topics, but the basic steps of the quest, as displayed in a toolbar at the top of the Web quest page, did not vary very much. Each of these explorations had an "introduction," which told about both the purpose and artistic context of the quest. Each also displayed a "tasks" menu, which expanded what would be required of students in greater detail, and then a "timeline" menu choice, under which the multiday projects were broken down by day, or group of days; under this menu choice the tasks in the "tasks" menu choice were also expanded upon, and slotted into the "timeline" breakdown of the project, giving students a precise idea of how progress should be measured.

Most worked in groups, although Motter specifically noted that she tried to be "flexible" on this point. Ultimately, the students—individuals or groups—were expected to create whatever art or presentation was required by the quest, and then post that on the class blog. This work was then available for the PSU art education students to critique, and provide their feedback, asynchronously, to Motter's student groups.

"I asked FHMS students to reflect on PSU students' feedback and consider it when creating future works. I also asked FHMS students to comment back to the PSU students by thanking them for their feedback, or asking questions," says Motter. She adds that in spring 2013, two Web quests offered students the chance to present their work using VoiceThread, a presentation tool that allows for voice-over annotation of slides.

All of this found its way into the local newspaper.

NETWORKING AND PROFESSIONAL DEVELOPMENT

Motter's summer breaks present an opportunity for her to pursue her own learning. She spent the summer of 2013 expanding her educational technology knowledge by taking two public university-level courses online: Educational Technology Leadership, and Deploying Information Technology Infrastructure. She also earned a state certification in K–12 technology education, while working toward her state instructional technology specialist certification. And she performed paid Web design work for a professor who teaches within PSU's College of Information Sciences and Technology.

Her own successful integration into the FMHS faculty, Motter attributes, in part, to the support of her assigned mentor, Kevin Lang. In speaking with me, Lang noted that, typically, a new teacher joining the faculty would be assigned a mentor teaching in the same discipline as the novice. However, given Motter's background and her being hired to build "a digital art program, within a fine arts department that was completely traditional," as Motter describes it, the mentoring arrangement made sense.

In Lang's view, Motter is achieving success with the program, in part because, in other classes, technology has become more commonly used—and having it available in an art class confirms and extends what students already experience in school. He also notes that technology brings differentiation to a discipline that previously seemed to reward only students with native, conventional artistic talent, for example, in drawing with watercolors, or sculpting with clay. "She's successful because students are not used to having this [technology in art class], so when she implemented Google SketchUp, and Doodles, and working with Penn State, and Skype, it was something that they took to right away, because students are used to seeing this [in other contexts]."

"This is art, too," says Lang. "It's not just taking a pencil and drawing, you can do art in many different ways. Not all students learn the same way. Some students, if you put a mouse in front of them, they can design a beautiful piece. But if you put a brush in front of them, they may not be able to paint well."

"In Forest Hills District, we're very blessed, we've got very supportive administrative staff and superintendent; they want to give the teachers the tech the teachers need . . . Here, at Forest Hills, it's a little different story; if we present something that we want to try, and we want to integrate, they're on board, and they allow them to try new things. If I go to a conference, and hear about something, they're very receptive," he notes. "There are pitfalls, it's naturally going to take time. We're redesigning the school. The only thing that is limiting right now, using the existing tech and software, is that there's a chain of command. However, if there's something that I want in my particular classroom, this is something that I feel our students would benefit from, and it would give them twenty-first-century skills, usually we say, 'Let's field test that and see what the results are . . . let's do it on a small scale . . . show results along the way," explains Lang. He says this approach was used in deploying a small number of iPads around the school with various teachers.

"We're in a rural area, a lot of times the school districts are far apart. In the last five years we've taken tours of different people and different schools to see what tech is being implemented. Other times, we have new teachers coming in, and they excel at certain kinds of software, and they can meet with teachers about the appropriate way to incorporate this technology," adds Lang. "What she does is, she says, 'Let's use the computers as a tool, but as a tool on how to present work, not just as a means to an end.' Maybe students will design with it, maybe they will sketch with it, maybe they will take pictures or create a slide show."

Motter participates in her discipline's ongoing public conversations about art education—and not just online. In 2013, she presented, with a panel, at both state and national art education conferences, on the topic of community activist art. At the 2013 NAEA Conference in Fort Worth, Texas, Motter and the panel presented on "Critical Community Art Project: Post Silence Activism." In Harrisburg, Pennsylvania, Motter and the same panel presented at the Pennsylvania Art Education Association Conference on the topic of "Post Silence: Community Activist Art." This past year [2014], Motter and a different panel discussed "Using Web 2.0 for Advocacy, Teaching, Collaboration, and Research," at the NAEA conference in San Diego, California.

Given her vocation, it makes sense that she would take a moment to participate in the art world. Last December, Motter also exhibited some of her own artwork, this time related to her dissertation work, a postcard community-based art project, at The Bottle Works Ethnic Arts Center, in Johnstown. For her, this is "my ongoing relational community artwork."

PLANNING FOR THE FUTURE

Motter has new projects planned—including more Web quests. And she has a new school to which she can look forward—one with lots of bells and whistles. She has been included in technology meetings for the new building project, which includes the design of two art rooms consisting of a room for two-dimensional art activities and one for three-dimensional art. And the hope is to develop a Mac-based lab for the art department.

She notes, "I use PowerSchool to enter my grades electronically, and most students regularly check their grades online. However, I would like to offer more detailed feedback on assignments. I post rubrics online for students to view, and students participate in online peer critiques by providing each other feedback at my course blog sites. I would like to be able to track students' comments more efficiently. Currently, I approve blog postings and scan them for student initials in order to give them credit for posting online. Ideally, I would like to use an online course management system, such as Penn State's ANGEL, that affords drop boxes for assignment submission and providing feedback," comments Motter. "I believe this would greatly help me with my organization and management of student projects, feedback, and grades. This is not currently the case at my school district."

Speaking of the limits of the technology to which she has access, Motter notes that "applications may have capability limits, but another technology can be found that surpasses the first's capabilities. I believe that tech integration for art education is limitless, as there is so much that can be explored and used for creative means. Tech integration opens up the field of art education to more possibilities for meaningful, creative, collaborative works."

What Motter also believes is that art education consists of a number of different pieces: connections based on personal experience, interest in the content, student motivation, hands-on learning, technological tools, and collaborative opportunities. For Motter, abundance or paucity of drawing skill, while important, should not stop students from interacting with the content in a way that provides meaningful learning opportunities, given the right kind of teaching and technology.

Keifer-Boyd notes that while Web quests and other uses of the Web have been explored extensively outside of art to foster critical and creative thinking among K–12 students, "art education wasn't really a part of that conversation," until now.

Lang observes that technology integration took a leap forward at FHMS when teachers were able to digitize and display lecture notes and assignment instructions in a variety of formats and within different venues; for instance, taking lecture notes, converting them to PDF files, or then displaying them from the teacher's computer on a smart board, as well as uploading them to the teacher's blog. He envisions more of this happening—for other teachers as well as Motter—in the future.

In general, says Lang, the school's incremental approach to technology integration has worked well. In "field-testing" iPads, teachers used a program called Notability to figure out how they could digitize, and more flexibly use and repurpose, classroom materials—such as lecture notes and handouts—by scanning the documents and putting them in the online storage program Dropbox.

"This is how we implemented the use of iPads," recalls Lang. And for students, "we started to have them do digital note-taking, create videos and submit them to competitions . . . twenty or thirty students trying them out."

"We don't put our eggs in one basket, but if the teachers are passionate about what they're doing with tech, then the district will make purchases," he says. "The biggest mistake is, teachers see something new and they immediately want to try it. Our approach [to technology] is to to take a step back, field-test it, go through the process. Not only do students understand it better, but teachers understand it better. It lessens the bite of learning new technology. Rather than jumping in, we do some research."

Recently, Motter wrote me an e-mail, saying, "I believe that technology's capability to connect art to other disciplines helps to maintain art's significance and relevance in the twenty-first century. The marriage of art and technology is becoming increasingly important in helping students obtain twenty-first-century skills such as communication, collaboration, creativity, innovation, and problem solving. Technology also helps to promote lifelong learning in the visual arts."

"Art is fluid and difficult to define. I don't think that technology is taking the focus away from art, but it is helping to push the boundaries of what we consider to be art," she remarks.

4

Championing Student Passions

Josh Stumpenhorst

SIXTH GRADE
ENGLISH LANGUAGE ARTS AND SOCIAL SCIENCE
Lincoln Junior High School, Naperville, Illinois

Josh Stumpenhorst centers his teaching around student passions and interests, using whatever technology is available to him—and he can gather up—to engage and inspire his sixth-grade students in English language arts and social science content. Applying what the International Society for Technology in Education (ISTE) called an "absolutely inspiring" style of teaching, Stumpenhorst has mined his own steadily growing online network to find new ways of engaging his students as a "creative leader" and "expert technologist," even as he shares the information and ideas he has gleaned with other teachers, both within and beyond his suburban Chicago-area school district.

His philosophy, and how it is executed in the classroom, have earned him awards, speaking engagements, and kudos from a range of organizations. Among them: Stumpenhorst was named Illinois Teacher of the Year in 2012 by his home state, as well as Educator of the Year by Illinois Computing Educators. Previously he was named one of several 2011 Emerging Leaders by ISTE. In 2013, he visited Brazil with other educators as a 2013 Pearson Foundation Global Learning Fellow. His book, A Whole New Teacher, *is being published by Corwin Press in 2014.*

STUMPENHORST TEACHES THREE periods of social science and a double-period block of English language arts. But whatever the class, whether they are reporting from ancient Rome in a mock-TV news segment, or responding online to thematic points in literature by video-recording their discussion of those points, students in his classes are always "demonstrating" what they know. Subject matter, posits Stumpenhorst, really has to connect with students over more than just "various dates and dead people."

"The best technology allows for individualized learning, and gives them a choice of format. It also allows them to access their passion, and eliminates the cookie-cutter approach," offers Stumpenhorst, noting that through his use of technology, "I have a huge expectation of independent work, and independent thinking."

This philosophy is what leads to a steady acquisition of technology and to students who can problem-solve both technical questions and questions about the content of their lessons, he asserts.

RAMPING UP

Initially, Stumpenhorst was able to purchase a cart of fifteen laptops through a grant from the local education foundation. He also has been able to obtain from the district a smart board, a document camera, a laptop for himself, and, through another grant, a computer for video editing—video is a big part of Stumpenhorst's curriculum. A colleague sought and obtained a grant for another cart of fifteen iPads, and so together they have a class set—the subject of coordination between the two each week, allowing for each class to get significant time with them.

He also has four different video cameras, including a Sony HD HandyCam. Some of the video camera equipment came from his taking over a semi-moribund computer club, after asking permission to do so, and then shifting the emphasis to video when the students in the club showed an interest in that medium. Each year the focus shifts due to changing student tastes, and Stumpenhorst just honors that by trying to obtain the necessary equipment, software, or access. For instance, through a National Education Association (NEA) grant, he was able to obtain a helmet cam for the club. This foray into extracurricular technology did not just yield some additional technology for his classroom; he has also learned a little more about how the children in his designated age group interact with the video. The new emphasis is on coding, based, again, on students' expressed interests.

Within his school, various initiatives have benefited his teaching practice, and he has also been a part of some initiatives to study and then promulgate certain types of technology, technology policy, and professional development throughout Lincoln. One initiative studied, and then implemented, has allowed students to "bring your own device" (known colloquially as BYOD). Devices range from smartphones to tablets to laptops. Another policy to encourage teachers to use social media in their professional development that Stumpenhorst—a big user of social media to learn about and share teaching ideas—worked on with a committee known as "The Brain Trust," has more recently been put on hold. The school district, says, Stumpenhorst, is reviewing "policies and procedures" related to this initiative. Meanwhile, Stumpenhorst continues to meet with teachers, share his knowledge, and coach when asked.

John David Son, the district's instructional technology director, notes that in looking at how smart boards were implemented, the district gradually has changed the way it implements technology. He noted that when smart boards were first made available, the interactive presentation boards were often used simply as "glorified whiteboards" by some teachers. To help model use of both the boards, and a range of other technologies, the district has begun taping technologically savvy teachers, like Stumpenhorst, and posting the videos on an internal site for teachers to download and view.

Son said last year: "Our district did a good job of putting a smart board in every classroom three years ago; we saw great uses of collaboration. However, some used it as a glorified whiteboard. I don't think we sent the right message, about how we envisioned them being used in the classrooms. For some, strictly for them, it's for presenting, and it's not a tool for kids to utilize. Some teachers thought, 'This is for me; the kids have their laptops.' So that was a lesson learned for us. We didn't do a good job."

"We have tech integration specialists in the district, teachers, who are released from duties; that was the first place we went, and had conversations, and talked about how we would remediate that. We were trying to make the most sense, pulled them together, talked to them about the best practices in the classroom. We found some videos, and on YouTube, and posted on TeacherTube, which modeled using smart boards," he said, adding that "one of our high schools is a smart showcase; there are smart certified teachers, and we're constantly looking at how do we bring along some teachers. We do have excellent internal resources."

With some of the hardware issues and access taken care of, Stumpenhorst focuses on bringing a variety of digital content to students, and making sure they understand how to use the technology so they can access it. He notes that students can be tripped up by details, in assembling an online slide show, video, or annotated podcast, when they try to find available files that are easily accessed, can be legally used in an educational presentation, and are connected to the kinds of activities the students are studying and upon which they are presenting. Because of this, he has become used to taking thousands of digital pictures on trips—especially any that involve flying—so that he has many images. As a result, he offers that he has a terabyte-sized hard drive "almost full" of images for use by his students. Although he expected to migrate many of these files to online storage, he is now encouraging his students to source images at the Wikimedia Web sites, which are copyright-free. Significantly, he knows he needs lots of free media available to his students if they are to create anything in his digitally infused curriculum.

"We've bought into Canvas" as an LMS (learning management system), notes Stumpenhorst. However, on Canvas, the YouTube player is blocked, so students posting their own videos cannot always watch them via Canvas. To solve this, Stumpenhorst will post videos on a personal YouTube channel that he set up, so they can watch their own videos—or something he has posted—at home. Students can also post a video to the network drive of the school's computer system, so that they can watch it as well.

Meanwhile, teachers are campaigning to get the YouTube player on Canvas unblocked. "If we continue to block this stuff, kids will never learn how to use it," Stumpenhorst says.

MATCHING LEARNING GOALS AND TECHNOLOGY

The technology director, Son, observes that Stumpenhorst makes all of his lessons "about the kids. Every tool that he utilizes, every activity that he utilizes, it's about the kids, and about their learning environment," says Son. "He ensures that the resources and tools and activities are aligned to standards, and it's not just about the standards. It's really about how the kids are actively engaged and the kids are creating authentic experiences, whether their learning experience is fun, interactive, or exciting."

For Stumpenhorst, "authentic" means an experience that connects to the students' real life in some way. Relative to Son's comments, there are two salient features of Stumpenhorst's teaching. First, students initially interface with a unit through the standard; he requires students, through a series of repeated procedures outlined in a graphic organizer they are given, to turn each standard into a question. Once they do that, they work through the answers to the question, then demonstrate those answers to that question in a way that connects with the student (such as a slide show, video, or podcast). Second, Stumpenhorst digitizes exam reviews by recording smart board unit reviews, and the simultaneous discussion, as screencasts, which are then uploaded. The student always has electronic links via Canvas to these two pieces of a unit: the samples of their responses to standards, and the notes from reviews.

Stumpenhorst: "I introduced the organizer to them in about the second third of the year. In the first third of the year, I model my lesson using it the same way. So in the first trimester, I always go through turning that standard into a question, and then producing 'my understanding of the content.' In the first trimester we do a lot more of this in whole-class. I introduce the organizer, we work through it together, and I model different examples of Step 4," which is the demonstration of content. "Anything I then ask them to do in demonstrating, later, we have already modeled, in terms of movies or podcasting," to demonstrate their understanding of the standard when it's time for them to do it on their own, Stumpenhorst explains. "When they start working this process on their own, they are working through the steps internally: 'What is your evidence of learning?,'" he continues.

For example, says Stumpenhorst, an Illinois standard in sixth-grade social studies is "Identify the contributions of China's first Emperor, Qin Shihuangdi." So students might respond with, "Question – What were Emperor Qin's contributions to China? What did he do that helped or hurt his people, and what overall impact did he have on China's history?"

He explains, "The question is the first step. Second step is answering the question using their book or other sources. Then they gather that information they have learned and produce their evidence. For this one they might make a poster with his contributions, or a simple essay," which they can do electronically or on paper.

Stumpenhorst takes the same approach in English language arts. "I introduce this process to them, and then I wean them off of me doing it for them, and they need to be working through it on their own." Ultimately, the students have "a good library of samples" to pull from. "They will be able to go back and look at these."

Says Stumpenhorst, "With anything I teach, my class is very choice-driven. Any project is learning how to show me what they know. We study Rome, from the republic to the empire. They have to find a way to demonstrate what they know about this to me. How would you do that? A podcast, perhaps. With any project, they have to know at the end, what they would do to demonstrate knowledge."

"The technical stuff, and learning that with them, can take time. They may say, 'I don't know how to do that,' so we go over it. I model a lot of stuff. Any project is learning about technology to some degree." Stumpenhorst builds in time to go over video technology. But he also recognizes that the variety of software and file types can be a stumbling block.

For reviews, "I will go over the notes on the [smart] board, and review a chapter of a book or a unit. I use Screencast-O-Matic; it provides a one-click record of everything I'm doing on the board, everything I'm writing. They then have a record of the screen, and any dialogue that occurred while we were talking about the notes," he says. Stumpenhorst further explains, "Screen capture is something I do anytime we are doing a class review. All of the content that was going to be on the test, we went through on the notes. Screen capture captured the dialogue and anything on the board." This is all uploaded to the Canvas platform.

One reason Stumpenhorst supports his students in finding ways to demonstrate their learning in an electronic format, or via the videotaping of a group discussion, is that "in my experience, with eleven- and twelve-year-olds, they can be pretty good about writing B.S. So this way, I know [that] they have to know what they are talking about."

He can also e-mail a link to this review to parents at home, with a message saying something like, "There is a test on China coming up."

FOSTERING COLLABORATION

Along with the expectation of independent work is an expectation that his students will also, when appropriate, collaborate with their fellow students, and if needed, help them—or seek them out, if necessary.

"I very strongly encourage group and collaborative work. If I'm up here at the front working with an individual student, I know that other kids are working on their own or with each other, if that is the task. I have to train them to actually work with each other effectively, because at the beginning of the year, they will often tell me, 'We're not allowed to talk to someone else.'"

Stumpenhorst likes his students to rely on each other, depending upon their skill sets and talents. "If they know Brad, over there, is good with Movie Maker [software], then they should know it's OK to consult Brad. Kids are smart, and they do pick up on who is good with something. They don't necessarily need me to rely upon," explains Stumpenhorst.

Although he likes students to produce their own video and audio presentations, "I don't let the kids get in front of a camera without a script, and without practicing for the reading of it; we do spend a lot of time on fluency. When we are talking about writing, I give them pretty strict time frames for video. When you only have two minutes with a camera, your writing must be succinct. There are kids that will write twenty pages, when two would do fine."

"Language arts is the best example" of choice in demonstrating knowledge, says Stumpenhorst. "Let's say we have as a standard, on theme or mood. They will select backdrops and themes and music, and how the characters relate to that theme. They might use iMovie trailers. On Mac, those are drag-and-drop. You have to come across, and get your point across. Music is a huge piece of it."

Regarding language arts in third trimester: "I'll have a document in there [online], between me and the kids; what that document will have is a listing of standards, and underneath they will describe what they are doing to show their mastery of conflict. They will respond with something like, 'I'm going to read these three pieces of text, and I will show how conflict is evident.' Or the evidence might be journal entries. So they have to do this three times. The beauty in Canvas is that it has a comment bar that is continuous. I have a dialog box, in which I can tell the student, 'You need to check this out,' such as a passage in a book, or a file online, that might help them understand something."

"What this means is that all those conversations that you might have at the [teacher's] desk can be archived," he adds.

DIFFERENTIATING

Differentiating is, by definition, something Stumpenhorst advocates and upon which he bases much of his teaching. In allowing his students to take control of a topic, through Internet research, say, he keeps them motivated and engaged.

Some of Stumpenhorst's assignments are not necessarily technology-intensive per se, such as a research paper. But, as Stumpenhorst frames the research paper project, it is likely to drive more intensive interaction with the Internet, and require teaching by Stumpenhorst, and discernment by the students, to understand the resources they are finding. Stumpenhorst calls his take on research papers "action research." The student writing such a paper has to look at the effect of one thing—a trend, phenomenon, situation—on the local community, home, or school, and must call for, and justify, some kind of action. Examples of this kind of paper, in his classes, have included the effects of gum-chewing on concentration, and the impact of listening to music on studying.

As he tells parents and students on his Web site, "Our focus will be on action research that will ultimately lead to a positive change." Explaining this, he says, "I'm not a huge fan of regurgitation; we do action research . . . Everything has to have a local impact in their home, community, or school, and they have to justify taking some action, in the paper." He notes that this is a good opportunity for him to increase the amount of student learning about properly crediting sources.

Occasionally he will create stations, or centers, in which students move about the room and perform specific activities, to learn about that content by interacting with the material or creating a product. "In social studies I do stations every once in a while. I did this one in Greece in geography; you could create a podcast, or they could go on Google Earth tour of ancient ruins, or they could listen to an audio, or a video, and just kind of take notes."

With any unit, Stumpenhorst provides a choice at the end. "At the end of a unit on early Chinese history they will tell me, 'I'm going to create a documentary of his life . . . I'm going to write an essay . . . I'm going to make a PowerPoint.'" With reading literature, Stumpenhorst often reaches out to his network via social media to find young adult fiction that would also be a fit for his class. Students have choices, but within a menu of books that Stumpenhorst has preselected.

"I access a couple of good lists, to what we call a 'mock Newbery list.' That's a list of young adult novels that could be potentially up for a New-bery award. I use books from my own experiences, and books that kids have recommended. I need to make sure they are district-approved."

"It's a step-by-step process. First of all, in terms of learning, what are the learning targets and outcomes? What do I want the kids walking away with? And then by myself I will reach out to the folks I know to find literature that is high-interest for my age group. I think I have a pretty good handle on this segment, but there are things I have never heard of."

Students may choose different books. Some students will choose the same ones, or will express interest in the same topic; Stumpen-horst tries to make reading groups contain students with similar in-terests. "I will give a quick synopsis. If I left the kids to make their groups, it's by friends, but if it's by interests, then they are more likely to make progress."

An example is, "We were talking about conflict. I modeled a mini-lesson with conflict, and then we had a short discussion. They then work on creating their demonstration, making some book trailers, some kind of skit, a play, that would be the process we would go through."

"We do a couple of different books during the year. I give them choices, within reasons, but I preselect. Some books are not on paper, but most are," says Stumpenhorst. "There is a cart of iPads in the build-ing. They have a really nice 'trailer' feature which takes the technical end off of it. Some will use Movie Maker, some kids have a Mac Pro and will use that."

With technology upgrades at school, he is able to widen the ways in which students access the material, whether books or other content. "We actually just upgraded all the wireless in our building to go BYOD.

I definitely know, because that is a part of the [BYOD] pilot. More of the kids are on their devices, when I want them to be on a device," he said.

ASSESSING

Self-assessment is woven into Stumpenhorst's pedagogy, whether it is through students providing "evidence" that they understand and have learned something, or demonstrating their learning with the results of a project they have put together on their own, or with a group.

Nevertheless, because standards underpin instruction, Stumpenhorst likes to put them in a document on Canvas, where students can continually refer to them. With multiple standards in play for each unit, he finds this is more useful for everyone than writing one standard up on a board or wall for each day of instruction—students may be working on multiple standards as part of a given project.

"I don't like rubrics," he tells me. "Teaching is often very subjective. In math and science, the rights and wrongs are very concrete. But in English and languages, nothing is more subjective than grading writing. We do have a learning target. And what I do is look at that project and what has been turned in. And that comes down to me. Being confident in the content, I will, upon looking at that project, be able to know what that kid knows."

"Because this kind of assessment can be subjective, that is why I require multiple pieces of evidence. They might contribute something other than that video. I tell the kids, 'Here are the questions I am going to ask you. This what you are going to be asked to do.' They get a copy of the learning targets, and the standards. There is no 'hiding things,' and they know what I'm after, and what they need to know"—referring to his posting of standards on the Canvas platform, for a given project.

And for the projects where Stumpenhorst establishes an online document with the standards, and how that student will meet those standards—that is "between me and the student," in which they have to explicitly state three ways they will show mastery. This document can be repeatedly referenced as a student navigates the activities. The three ways might include three different journal entries with different examples of one type of plot device, for instance. Or it might be a podcast that records the student explaining his understanding of the learning that needs to have taken place; a video would also suffice.

"Otherwise, if they show it one time, and they nail it, it may be a fluke," he commented.

When it comes to grading writing projects, Stumpenhorst uses the comment bar feature in Canvas to perform what he calls "small-snapshot" grading. It sets up a visible dialogue between the teacher and the student. This, to some extent, reflects both a desire to utilize the efficiencies of online writing as much as a philosophy about how writing ought to be graded. He will "jump in" to a student's rough draft multiple times, offering a comment on individual issues or problems raised by the writing—for example, an issue of tense, or usage, or a point of analysis.

"In some ways, I grade more, not less, but it's small-snapshot," comments Stumpenhorst. "I can give kids comments ten or twelve times, but by the third time, I know [the writing], and I don't have to read it fresh. Or, did they take the feedback, and do something with it? It's so much more efficient, it does not take me very long to make a comment," explains Stumpenhorst. "One of the mistakes I often see with teachers is that they put too much commentary. For the most part, kids can only work on one thing at a time. It's small, isolated doses of criticism. Just one thing, rather than ninety-two things."

Along with many teachers, Stumpenhorst does use peer editing and peer feedback. He provides a peer-revision checklist to the students, and gives them questions that target specific issues cropping up in most papers: are the verbs in the correct tense? Is there an accurate use of singular and plural words? If they are using Microsoft Word, he will ask them to insert comments into the document, using the New Comment feature. And he also asks the students to mark issues: "Circle it, or highlight it in yellow."

While parents can log in, using Canvas, to see assignments, Stumpenhorst will happily e-mail them a link to an assignment, or even excerpts from a research paper or writing sample that is proving troublesome for the student to complete. Students can send their work to Stumpenhorst in many different ways: they can save it to the network drive for the school, or they can send documents in Canvas, via a message, or they can also post it in Canvas to the specific assignment's site within the LMS.

FOSTERING DIGITAL LITERACY

"We use a variety of tech skills in writing and reading, and that runs the gamut, too. For some of our novice tech users, just navigating to the Office Suite, and opening up Publisher, and creating a brochure, is a challenge. But they need to understand how these things work, and when you download something, where does it go," notes Stumpenhorst.

Example: "When kids bring in a QuickTime file on their iPhone, and we're using PCs . . . they need to know how to convert that file," says Stumpehhorst, adding that "I try to expose them to a lot of open-source technology. There's so much garbage out there, and this is also a tech skill and a literacy skill" to understand how to manipulate various file types. He makes sure to teach aspects of hardware literacy, too—for instance, about the recorders built into computers, and how to create a podcast using that recorder.

Digital literacy is critical learning for these students; as Stumpenhorst puts it, "They know how to get to Wikipedia, and they don't know how to make sense of what they've found."

NETWORKING

Stumpenhorst discusses his practice and ideas about education at his blog, StumpTheTeacher.blogspot.com. He examines a range of issues—from his opinion about various pedagogical initiatives, to a recapping of his attendance and speaking engagements at different educational conferences, such as the Staff Development for Educators Conference in Chicago, in the summer of 2013. There he spoke about project-based learning and "student-driven learning with technology," sharing firsthand experiences, and a video that one of his students had created about John Paul Jones, the eighteenth-century American naval hero.

Some of these presentations, and his pedagogy and curricular choices, draw upon his work as a team member of a sixth-grade social science curriculum design team. When administrators realized several years ago that the current grading system was not working, Stumpenhorst and a social science curriculum committee on which he served developed a transition for himself and other teachers to standards-based grading. He and the committee investigated the standards-based grading model that they ultimately designed and implemented. "I changed the grading system in my class and helped a handful of other teachers do the same. I still do serve on the social science curriculum committee," explains Stumpenhorst.

Instructional technology director Son says: "Our curriculum is written across the technology. We have teachers that use it in varying degrees. Another strategy that we have worked on with teachers [is] observing [via video recording] other teachers teaching effectively with technology, and we've posted them [the videos]." Son then advises teachers, "If you want to learn about it, watch video about engaged learning."

He adds, "That means getting teachers the time to watch proficient teachers deliver quality lessons, and bring it back and try it in their classroom. We're starting to do this, giving teachers time to go into classrooms, using our LMS . . ."

"Through Josh's leadership, and his PLN [personal learning network], he is a big advocate of social media and social networking, whether that's using his blog or Twitter. We want our teachers to create their own PLNs, to build knowledge with teachers all over the world, how he's used these tools to bring new ideas into his own classroom," remarks Son.

Stumpenhorst first became involved in using Twitter as a resource when he joined that platform's Monday night social studies–focused chats with other educators; his involvement with social media as both a source of ideas, and a way to share his own, just took off from there.

Although Son had hoped to use Josh's expertise and experience to model for other teachers how to use Twitter, for instance, that effort is on hold for now. "The 'brain trust' about social media—we've been shut down," Stumpenhorst reports. Higher-ups in the district were not yet comfortable with "protocols and procedures" in place for teachers to do this kind of networking.

Meanwhile, Stumpenhorst continues to do a lot of educational consulting and training outside the district, as well as serving as a regional consultant for Mind Gamez LLC, and specifically its History Heroes game. And, outside of his classroom is where he also garners ideas from sources and experts; at a conference, for instance, he might tweet a request for information to tinker with a presentation, or to obtain some information for curricular edits.

Lincoln has run Innovation Days in the past, where students get to work on a favorite project for the entire day, and then show that work off to their class. Stumpenhorst developed these in concert with the school and other teachers, after becoming inspired by Daniel Pink's 2009 attention-grabbing treatise on motivation and management, *Drive: The Surprising Truth About What Motivates Us*. The book argues against external punishment and reward paradigms, and for "autonomy, mastery, and purpose" as more sustainable and meaningful drivers of human behavior. Pink later mentioned Stumpenhorst and his project on his own blog, providing some vindication for the risk of upending the school's schedule to experiment with activities Stumpenhorst believed would inspire students and help them see school as a place of exploration for their particular talents and interests.

Trips and conferences have also generated teaching ideas. Stumpenhorst developed a lesson outline about global unrest based on his trip to Brazil, which he then posted on BetterLesson.com, a free lesson-sharing Web site, as did other participating NEA fellows. The lesson outline asks students, through guided questions and other activities, to examine, contrast, compare, and analyze ancient (for example, Roman) and modern forms of unrest—including the 2013 public protests in São Paulo,

Brazil, and other areas of the country, along with turmoil resulting from the Arab Spring.

REFLECTING

ISTE praised Stumpenhorst as a teacher who "shares resources with his colleagues in his district and around the world." Within Lincoln, Stumpenhorst is described by parents and colleagues as a passionate teacher who constantly develops innovative ways to motivate students. Parents also appreciate his ability to help students navigate the social and emotional challenges of junior high.

Given these appraisals of Stumpenhorst's teaching, the comments of Illinois' superintendent of schools seem to evaluate correctly what Stumpenhorst does—and achieves—in the classroom:

"Josh is a student-centered teacher who focuses on creating effective learning that will help every student be successful. His ability to reach students of all skill levels engages them and inspires his colleagues," said State Superintendent Christopher A. Koch, upon awarding Stumpenhorst the state's Teacher of the Year award in 2012. "Josh also shares his teaching strategies via an online professional learning network that he created. His educational blogs reach thousands of educators across the globe and demonstrate his leadership skills as well as his continuous efforts to be the best for his students."

Of his pedagogy, Stumpenhorst opines, "The passion that kids have is often never covered; tech allows them to access their passion."

5

Creating Something New

Laura Bradley

EIGHTH GRADE
ENGLISH LANGUAGE ARTS/DIGITAL MEDIA
Kenilworth Junior High School, Petaluma, California

Laura Bradley began teaching in an era of chalkboards and overhead projectors, but all that changed when she went back to school to get her master's degree, after teaching English to junior high school students for eighteen years. Since then, her practice has undergone considerable change: she co-created a digital media class, becoming a lead technology integrator at her school and within the district. With another teacher, she is managing the student-run television station.

Bradley is in her third year of hosting an online novel-writing program in her eighth-grade English classes. Her digital media class continues to enter their apps into competitions. And she encourages her students to engage in literary analysis through a blogging format. Slowly, she is introducing more digitally-based assessments into her classroom. Yet she remains skeptical of totally paperless pedagogy, and mindful of the digital divide: Kenilworth Junior High School is the only Title 1 school in her district, which, she says, is a reminder that levels and degrees of technology access at home are unequal across the school's student body.

In 2005, she earned her National Board Certification. In 2012, she earned her master of arts in curriculum, teaching, and learning from Sonoma State University. That same year, Bradley's writing pedagogy garnered national notice when a student of Bradley's wrote about her writing experience in Bradley's class, in a piece published in the New York Times. *Last year, she became a Google Certified Teacher.*

RAMPING UP

The initial hardware for Bradley's classroom came—as with so many teachers—from local foundation grants she sought out on her own. As someone who taught herself much of the technology she uses, and who understands what her age group does and does not know about academic technology use, Bradley values, and emphasizes in her teaching, basic digital literacy skills as much as she does moving students toward working intensively on digital platforms.

With her principal, Emily Dunnagan, and the district as a whole revising curricula to meet Common Core goals, the idea of pushing the work of learning onto students and of having them share their learning experiences with each other has become more important—more reflective of Common Core values. Bradley trains other teachers in a variety of settings, both on her curriculum choices and on the district's technology platform, which is now Google Apps. Even as she sings the praises of Google Docs, which her students are using for writing practice, she reveals her traditional side as she talks about her concerns for the continued teaching of novels, essay writing, and penmanship—all contentious content in the discussion about what twenty-first-century English language arts should look like. And she speaks of that traditional concern of eighth-grade teachers, but pitched to twenty-first-century students: preparing her students adequately for both high school work, in general, and using technology in a productive and appropriate way, in particular. Despite this, Bradley describes herself as "definitely not a techie."

For her, "tech" can enrich learning: "Kids can use technology to create something new. That's one of the most valuable and profound uses of technology—creating a book trailer, for example, and combining images and words. English used to be just writing, and communication is so much more visual . . . communication that can create sound, effects, images, and moving images."

"There's just so much more potential to be creators, not just users," she adds.

From talking to Bradley it sounds as if she spends almost as much time educating herself as she does educating her early-teen students. Some of that comes from necessity—the incremental, stop-start progress of technology integration results from working in a state faced with near-constant turmoil in public school funding. She began her exploration of educational technology with almost no available hardware.

Her educational technology journey commenced prosaically, just over five years ago, when she began navigating coursework for her education master's degree at a nearby California State University campus, Sonoma State. Bradley's educational technology professor, Jessica Parker, encouraged students to try small bits of technology in their classrooms, even without the necessary classroom infrastructure: in Bradley's case, that meant having the students blog on school library computers.

Bradley's first attempts to do this a few years back were messy, with her trying to help students set up Google accounts and e-mail in order to use Google's Blogger Web site. Account setup required cell phone verification, but at that time some students did not own phones, did not bring them to school, or could not access the setup procedure.

She persisted, by writing a grant to the local educational foundation for Petaluma schools. Ultimately, that earned her fifteen laptops, and then another fifteen a short while later—giving her, essentially, a class set. Meanwhile, regional education authorities sought out Bradley to test Moodle, a platform on which teachers can put all sorts of materials—syllabi, exams, documents, and other learning materials—while also providing a place for some interactivity, such as blogging.

Knowing that it might take some time to work through the learning curve for Moodle, she ultimately decided to try it in a lower-track

English class, which she taught in a daily time slot that, practically speaking, stretched over two periods. This experience gave Bradley an understanding of how she might move some functions, lessons, and activities onto a virtual platform. Meanwhile, Dunnagan asked Bradley to create an elective digital media class, and that has served as a piece of Bradley's personal professional development learning lab.

For Bradley, incorporating technology is a multistep process, the first of which is straightforward, and the second less so. First, she figures out how a program works—something that she is always seeking out other resources to support her in doing, whether from a network of other teachers online, school colleagues, county education office technology experts, or corporations, like Google. Second, Bradley figures out how to weave it into her curriculum so it benefits student learning outcomes. For her, this process weighs her standards, her aims, knowledge of her age group, and her interest in promoting digital literacy in this last year of school, before the demands of high school.

But, for other kinds of activities, Bradley is not yet sold on the idea of junking low-tech. Every year she buys 150 spiral notebooks, on sale, so that her students can journal. Previously, with only half a set of classroom computers, this made sense. "We still do plenty of writing that doesn't require multiple drafts," notes Bradley. "Are we going to pull out the [computer] cart every time we journal or take notes? For the first time, I have been thinking, 'Maybe we could do that online.' It's an ongoing shift in my mind. Before, we'd take them out for a special purpose, and then we would take them out more, and so I'm in transition between paper and online."

Recently she has traded the laptops she garnered via grants, with Dunnagan, for a district-funded class set of MacBook Airs, the Apple laptop. The original set of laptops is now being used by another Kenilworth class. These are kept at school, and students do not take these laptops home. So Bradley is careful about the way she assigns work, in order to forestall any issues of computer and Internet access that may arise if a student does not possess that access at home. Progress on a related front promises flexibility, however: the 2012–2013 school year was the first year in which students were provided e-mail accounts as part of the district adopting Google Apps, which meant that Bradley did not have to walk her students through opening e-mail accounts.

FOSTERING DIGITAL LITERACY

The idea that kids are "digital natives" is a myth, claims Bradley. Her kids are indeed playing games on their phones and using social media to communicate and re-mix media to suit their needs and interests. But these behaviors do not necessarily mean they are instantly prepared to use digital platforms to engage with, and create, academic work that also meets state standards, while using these tools, she comments.

Thus, she has discovered that the fact that her students furiously text on smartphones does not necessarily indicate that the texting student has any more knowledge of how to create an online account than anyone else—child or adult. Writing on a screen does not immediately make students better writers, she notes.

"For the first time, this [past school] year [2013–2014], students all had accounts provided by the district. But they still don't know how to use them, so we spend time on that. I actually give them e-mail assignments, like 'Send me an e-mail and tell me about the book you are currently reading. Include characters, conflict, etc.' And then we have to talk about how to compose an e-mail to a teacher, as opposed to a text to a friend," observes Bradley.

She continued, "It's very interesting: sometimes I feel like when it's a Google Doc, they write more, and it looks better, but I've also been surprised at how many of them don't proofread. It has to be taught, and they're not better at it, just because it's electronic."

Bradley says she recognizes that any lessons, activities, or interactivity she is able to build into her curriculum are really doing double duty: addressing a curriculum standard, and content schedule, as well as a literacy skill that transcends the content, and that can be used both in her class later on, and in, other classes in her students' futures. For example, one approach might be making sure students know how to add a cite (or how to get a search tool to create an automatic citation, which some are capable of) for an image they hope to embed in a presentation or on-line essay. Incorporating certain formal language in a blogged response to another student is another skill she works on with students, although Bradley notes that she has always taught this kind of skill in one form or another: "This is something I've always done, whether online with kids or in class discussions or peer feedback on papers—they need the language of discussion/feedback/response/critique, etc. So I provide sentence frames . . . to help them write an academic response. We practice in class discussions and lit groups as well as on the blogs," she wrote me in an e-mail.

Digital literacy gets a boost, Bradley learned, when more than one teacher is working to integrate a particular skill—such as digital presentations or blogging—into the curriculum. Bradley found this out when instituting a new kind of final examination that required student groups to assemble during class a presentation online. Science and social science teachers are requiring students to more often create presentations using software, rather than construction paper or poster board, and Bradley believes this is echoed in her students' dexterity with presentation programs like PowerPoint.

MATCHING LEARNING GOALS WITH TECHNOLOGY

"I always want to know: how will this help them write better—what effect will it have?" asks Bradley, rhetorically. When and how much technology to integrate into a curriculum that she has spent years setting up, and which matches up to voluminous California standards, is a continual interior debate for Bradley.

It starts with units like *The Pearl*, a John Steinbeck novella that has been required for years. Taking place in Mexico's Baja California region, and set within a different time and culture, the book can be challenging for middle school–age students, says Bradley. For a lower-track class, with which she was piloting the Moodle platform, teaching the novella presented some opportunities for students to more meaningfully connect with the book, using technology. The Moodle platform provided a virtual "home" for the class, where Bradley could place links to unit materials and to communication tools, such as blogs.

Although students read a hard-copy version of the book, they were also able to view contextual videos and material on this Moodle site. The videos provided information about the geographic area in which the book takes place and about pearl-diving and the local culture. Bradley decided to go this route, knowing that a one-time whole-class viewing might yield a discussion after the fact. But, on the other hand, posting a video online would allow her students the ability to view it repeatedly, and potentially from outside the classroom. It's availability provided security for students, and helped them take ownership of the unit's material, she recalls, by taking notes on the video, on their terms.

For literary analysis, Bradley chose to use a blog, striking a middle ground between, on the one hand, dictating how and what students would post on the blog and, on the other, a free-for-all. With her guidance, the blog then became a tool for students to teach each other, and helped them develop some deeper expertise—both about the book and about blogging. "I wanted them all to be able to read one another's analysis, since they were all different," she explained.

Using the blog, students chose what aspect of *The Pearl* they wanted to write about—but importantly for Bradley—from a list of literary concepts Bradley provided online, such as conflict, character development and motivation, influence of setting, figurative language use, and theme.

Adds Bradley, in an e-mail to me, "I've always had students choose what to write about in response to the literature because my goal is to get them to think as they read. If I feed them questions, it's like I'm telling them what to notice." She continued, if the blog is used this way, "then they turn in all these different responses, and so I want them to see one another's [responses] and talk about their analysis—share what they noticed, respond to what someone else noticed, etc."

For this, and for other units where technology became a central teaching tool, Bradley says she became the "screenshot queen," to visually model, via handouts, where she wanted students to go at each step. She used both newspaper and online resources to discuss inappropriate blog postings, general online technical skills, the nature of online discussion prompts, staying on top when responding to blog posts, making sure avatars for online accounts did not include a personal photo, and that they stuck to using first names only.

She provides detailed instructions for blogging. "Kids won't blog just because there is a blog there, much like they won't write just because there is paper—they need specific assignments, directions, expectations, due dates, etc., just like they do with any other assignment. So although my students choose what to write about with regard to literature, I give them clear expectations for what analysis should look like, how much they need to write, and when each piece is due. And then when they are required to post on the blog, they are also given directions for how to respond to their peers. I'm a bit obsessive about fairness, so I don't just say, 'Respond to any post.' I have the kids choose names out of a hat to respond to so that everyone gets responses, and then they are free to respond to more if they want. And that's where the engagement often kicks in—they aren't required to comment on more, but they often do, and the conversations continue from there, in blog threads," explains Bradley.

Continuing this point: "Three years ago, I had them do a lot of reflecting on a blog, for my master's work. They said, 'Oh my gosh, I tried so much harder because I knew my friends would see it,' and this sort of thing," adds Bradley. "You have to make it an assignment to go to the blog. And often, in an assignment, to go back to the journals afterward. A lot of them said, 'This student showed me something I had not considered.' The ability to learn about something from the literature was significant, from this other student . . . There could be thirty different responses and ideas about the book. They're pulling whatever in the book interested them, that's why I want them to see everyone else's responses."

The online responses of adults to real-world products also provide lesson material. Teaching satire as a literary form can be tough at first; it's a mature form of humor and social criticism. To help students enter into this world in a way that is both accessible, and promotes digital skills, Bradley sought to use snarky product commentary that purchasers often use on major online store sites, familiar to many—in this case, Amazon.com.

"When a product is offered that may not be the most necessary product—like the banana slicer—clever Amazonians will write satirical reviews, praising the wonders of the silly device. I showed those reviews to my students as a way for them to learn satire, and then we watched a dozen infomercials for very silly products. They wrote their own satirical reviews for the products and posted them on our own satirical banana blog, and then they had great fun reading each other's reviews," e-mailed Bradley.

Whatever the online assignment, Bradley insists that, regardless of how much student choice is built into the task so as to foster ownership of it, it is important to set out clear guidelines. She says she has sometimes encountered teachers who are disappointed when they assign students to blog about something on a class blog, and they end up not doing it in a way that is relevant—or even not doing it all.

Dunnagan observes that Bradley succeeds by integrating not just the technology, but the "four Cs of the Common Core"—communication, creativity, collaboration, and critical thinking.

"Which is really just 'good teaching,'" remarks Dunnagan.

DIFFERENTIATING AND ENCOURAGING INDEPENDENCE

It is therefore no surprise when Bradley observes, "Middle school students respond best to assignments that offer a balance of choice and direction." Her task is providing both, but increasingly allowing both the individual choices and the directed learning to take place online, or in some format that can be shared, which she finds valuable as a teaching tool, as it shifts some of the learning onto students and encourages student-to-student interaction. One activity Bradley champions is a weeks-long novel-writing exercise, part of a national instructional effort by a nonprofit organization. The activity, known as National Novel Writing Month (nicknamed NaNoWriMo), which combines online writing with traditional paper-based modes of instruction, fits into Bradley's aims for teaching technological literacy, basic creative writing, and long-form writing structure. Because it makes use of Google Docs and e-mail, Bradley likes the idea of providing this kind of latitude, which allows her to further help her students get comfortable with online writing, online editing, peer editing, and communicating with other students not in their class about schoolwork.

"There is the writing part and then there is the tech part—but they are woven together," says Bradley, who has blogged on this subject. "They need to be familiar with Gmail and Google Docs, so we learn those applications in September–October," says Bradley. The nonprofit running the project provides a paper-based planning packet, which Bradley supplements with her own rubric. Students then read one novel as a class very early in the school year while they are readying their technical skills. During this time, Bradley works with students on language arts standards like character development, and then they analyze together how the author of the class novel accomplished the writing of the novel.

"Then students use Google Docs, too, so that they can get used to how they work. They do a timed writing in a doc so they can get a sense of what an appropriate word goal would be—so they learn how to check word counts in a doc. We do a shared doc for all students to see, where they insert their novel synopsis—so they learn how a shared doc works, and they get a peek into others' stories," explains Bradley.

"After that, students create accounts on the NaNoWriMo site, which is like a social network site, so as they are learning how to write a novel and how to be part of an online writing community, they are also learning appropriate social network behavior—it's similar to Facebook. They also learn how to navigate a site," explains Bradley. "I continue to be amazed at how many of them just look at the page but don't do anything with it. It's like they have to be told, 'Click here! Try clicking there! Read what's on the screen and explore!' They just aren't familiar with navigating online sites. I actually see the same when I am training teachers who are not active online; they just don't know how to explore."

Continuing, she explicates, "I teach them about having more than one tab open. And the plan for 'NaNo time' is that they log in to Gmail first, then open a new tab and log in to their NaNo account; just that is new for many of them: opening extra tabs. They learn that they can be working on a doc, and then jump over to another tab to find resources, inspiration, etc. That's a twenty-first-century skill, right? Multiple tabs for academic work."

Adds Bradley, "The beauty of all the prep we do prior to NaNo is that many of them start saying, 'Can I start my novel yet?' I can say with certainty that eighth graders do not ask for permission to write. They also say, 'Is it OK if I work on my novel at home?' So much time is devoted to preparation that they are chomping at the bit when November 1st arrives."

COLLABORATION AND ASSESSMENT

Like all teachers, grading for Bradley has often proven to be a labor-intensive, time-intensive activity. After she obtained Google teacher certification, Bradley began casting about for ways to use that platform to assess her students more efficiently, and get a better sense of the status of their learning. She also found that by pushing into digital assessment territory, she could address more standards than she might with "butcher block paper and magic markers."

On a formative level, Bradley took a critical look at how much grading she was doing, and how well that grading was affording, or not affording her, insights into how much her students were learning, and how much they were comprehending assignments—especially independent ones—as well as whether her students were making progress toward certain milestones.

Typically, in middle school English, students are often required to choose and read a book independently, and then create a report on that book that draws out certain aspects of standard structure; these days students also create slide shows or videos that provide this information in the form of a "trailer"—much like a movie trailer that promotes a film's high points, key characters, and snippets of evocative dialogue.

Some percentage of students may not complete the assignment on time, that is, finish their book and leave enough time to summarize and analyze its contents. Moreover, even if they do finish their book, they may not draw out any of the information requested. Heretofore, the results of this kind of assignment have often been gleaned only at the end, when the assignment is presented to the class, or turned in for credit. Bradley decided to extract a few of her own questions she normally asks in student conferences or through interim paper quizzes, and put these into a form that would allow the students to answer a series of questions online, and then submit it electronically.

"They use Google Docs to write (allowing for easy sharing, collaborating, peer editing, etc.), they post (and respond to) literary analysis on a blog, and they report back to me via Google forms," Bradley says.

"I see much better turn-in rates when I use [online Google] forms via e-mail, but probably, partly, because we do that in class. I don't send forms as homework because I don't want to have to address the issue of kids without access at home," says Bradley. "But I also think the students perform better with a form because they just tend to write more if they are at a laptop. Writing on paper seems to bring out the minimalist in them."

It also meant that students had a written record of where they were in their progress that persisted, could be shared with their parents, and provided self-regulatory information as they balanced all of their assignments. Bradley found creating it fairly easy; she used some of her newly acquired knowledge as a Google Certified Teacher.

Final assessments are another grading headache for teachers, and a studying headache for students, often encouraging them to memorize information and regurgitate it the next day. Bradley decided she could take the risk of piloting a different idea, which would involve students working in groups, obtaining individual grades for their participation and for individual tasks within the group, and sharing information—something she felt they would enjoy, and also benefit from, in thinking about the tasks. It would also use an extra-long class period, typically scheduled before winter break, for final examinations.

"I wanted them to be able to talk about the themes with each other, because they would come up with much richer results. In addition, because they could search in the Internet, find and embed relevant images in their presentations, it also covered several standards at once, including 'understanding symbolism' and 'digital presentation of ideas,'" remembers Bradley. "I like to have something that day that pulls together big ideas from the semester and sends them home with a stronger understanding of what they've learned."

The class had read *The Moves Make the Man*, a Newbery Award–winning novel about, among other things, racism. Then, they had examined other media-related themes: movies like *Unconquered* and *For One Night*, along with poems such as "Invictus." She wanted groups to identify themes connecting the media, with each student responsible for a different aspect of the connecting theme—and a different slide in their digital presentation. She physically cut a copy of "Invictus" into couplets, and put them in a bowl. Groups would work on the couplet and the theme connecting it to the other media, based upon which couplet they drew from the bowl. To set this up, Bradley identified groups within her class; to save time, she moved desks together and took laptops from the cart and put them on desks. She wrote directions for one group member, and that one person with the directions created the blank version of the presentation, shared it with the group members, who then could all contribute to making the final version. Using Google Docs, that group leader then shared their doc with the members of other groups. Then Bradley distributed general directions to the class outlining what they needed to do to create acceptable content for their slides.

After that, students identified a couplet in the text; they next identified what theme was expressed in that couplet, and then found evidence of that theme in the other works (book, movies, poem). Each student then created a slide that included the title of a text, an explanation of how the theme is evident in the text, and a symbolic image to represent the theme. Students all had laptops, so all group members worked simultaneously on the presentations.

Bradley recalls that some "hilarity ensued as they discovered they could edit one another's slides as they worked; made for some great work on cooperating and collaborating, trying to piece together a presentation that was unified yet allowed for their individual styles."

"As each student presented their slide with their group, to the class, I marked a rubric for his or her identification of theme, explanation of the theme in other works, choice-slash-explanation of symbolic image in slides, and projection of voice and eye contact as he or she spoke," explains Bradley.

NETWORKING

Midway through Bradley's graduate degree work, the district hired Dunnagan to be principal. Bradley says this was important in increasing support for technology integration at the school: Dunnagan worked in the high-tech sector early in her career and had obtained a master's in educational technology. Soon, Dunnagan asked Bradley and another teacher to design a digital media elective, which Bradley now teaches.

"At every school I've worked at there are the go-getters. But more importantly, if you let them go and do things, other teachers become less nervous about trying new things, and then they, in turn, become proselytizers," remarks Dunnagan, who views part of her job as making sure teachers can find the time to pursue more of the technology training they want, and need. She's happy to help teachers reclaim even small bits of time—ten minutes here, a class period there. Whether substituting for a teacher, or changing after-school supervisory obligations, she describes efforts to create space for teachers to educate themselves or other teachers about technology, or to learn from those who are already technology-savvy. "I have a huge brain trust of teachers," says Dunnagan. "The question is, how do we share knowledge in a way that is useful?"

It took two tries to get in, but Bradley made it into Google's elite professional development program for teachers. So in the summer of 2013, Dunnagan sent Bradley to the Google program; Bradley felt that it was geared less for teachers than for school and district technologists—a role she has even considered taking. But taking on such a role would mean that she would not be teaching, which is her first love. Still, at the intensive sessions, Bradley says that she garnered many tips and tricks geared toward optimizing use of various Google apps.

Bradley has also obtained funds to go to other conferences and meetings. She grabs ideas from teachers online, like Bradley Lands, Kevin Brookhouser, Catlin Tucker, and Alice Keeler, "who put out lots of help for teachers on Twitter, YouTube, and their Web sites, so I find them especially useful. The Google community in general is amazing. In preparation for a workshop for my staff on Google Drawing, I put out a question on Google+ for help. Right away, lots of Google teachers responded, and I've never met most of them."

"Recently I discovered Zachary Walker of *The Last Backpack* [blog]— he has posted some of my tech stories, and I learn from his posts, too. And I still go to the English Companion Ning [Web site] quite often, although more to share my perspective than to get help from others. As much as I love all the new tech teaching strategies, I still love to talk specific language arts curriculum, w/ or w/o tech. Just being connected online continues to bring me great ideas—I have been subscribing to the Accomplished Teacher by SmartBrief [Web site]for many years, plus now I glean from Edutopia, ISTE [International Society for Technology in Education], and CUE [Computer-Using Educators] resources, and of course all those Google teachers. Since these pop into my e-mail inbox—or Facebook feed—I am reminded to see what's there," recounts Bradley.

"NaNoWriMo is still top of my list . . . I'm still finding new ways to teach it. And since all our English 8 teachers do NaNoWriMo now, we share ideas and tweak the program together. Plenty of #NaNoWriMo tweets—it's a big community."

"Teachers who tweet are great," Bradley continues. "I find lots of ideas there from a wide range of teachers. And my own Twitter following has grown enough that when I tweet now, I usually pick up a couple new followers each time. I did a blog post recently about how valuable it is to network this way—it's the current version of 'stealing teachers' good ideas when they leave their original document on the copy machine.' Ironically, the idea I blogged about came from a hard-copy edition of a teacher magazine—that's still a good resource."

PLANNING FOR THE FUTURE

Bradley will renew her National Board Certification this year. As a component of that process now focuses on technology, she has much to include that she did not include in her application packet the last time she went through the process. And, she has taken up the cry to promote a coding club, after seeing how much fun her students had participating in something called an "Hour of Coding," sponsored by Computer Science Education Week.

But, she has found that advising on the television station with a fellow teacher is one project too many. Instead, she's proposed to the district a new English class, which would take over the TV program as permanent part of an advanced eighth-grade English class, focused on digital journalism. Meanwhile, she continues to stay in touch with the movement promoting software coding in schools through her teaching of the digital media class.

"The class is an example of how kids today don't have to rely on teachers in order to learn—there are so many tutorials and help sites online, they can learn practically anything on their own," Bradley observes. "Although I'm a little uncomfortable with my inability to actually teach some of what my students are doing in my class—such as writing code—I am sure this is the future: we need to teach kids how to take advantage of all those resources, rather than think teachers are the only ones who hold the knowledge they need."

6

Guiding the Experience

Christopher Craft

SIXTH GRADE, STEM
CrossRoads Middle School, Columbia, South Carolina

Nationally recognized for his teaching, Christopher Craft is a big proponent of individualizing learning, and of guiding the learning experience of students, whether they are working on their own or with other students. And although he's been recognized for his efforts in using technology within his teaching practice, Craft is firm in his belief that "technology is always subservient to really good pedagogy."

Craft was named an Emerging Leader in 2010 by the International Society for Technology in Education. The National School Boards Association's Technology Leadership Network named Craft one of "20 to Watch" for the 2012–2013 school year. In his STEM classes (science, technology, engineering, and mathematics), technology is a tool to create other tools, such as cell phone apps and robots, and to do so in a way that connects deeply with his students' personal interests as well as their personalities

Craft is well suited to teach both: he obtained his bachelor of arts in Spanish from the University of South Carolina in 2008. He went on to obtain a master of arts in education from his alma mater in 2010, before obtaining his doctorate in 2011. He has also obtained certification from the National Board for Professional Teaching Standards in 2013. Craft speaks widely, and has keynoted several education conferences, including Powering Up with Technology in Prince George's County, Maryland, and Google in Education North Carolina Summit, both in 2013.

RAMPING UP

Beginning in the fall of 2013, Craft began focusing solely on STEM instruction; prior to this, he also taught world languages. CrossRoads is devoted exclusively to sixth graders. Students at CrossRoads arrive there at the beginning of the year, having gone to various elementary schools in the district. At the end of the year, they go on to a middle school that serves seventh and eighth graders. A single-gender option exists for students for four core content classes; common time and exploratory classes are co-ed. The school uses a variety of technology platforms, including Google, Haiku, and Edmodo, but does not designate one as an official learning management system. Craft has taught himself to use all of them, in varying degrees. He notes that while the school has not always had a dedicated technology support staff, which he calls a "weird little gap," it has not stopped him from either figuring out programs on his own, or getting help when he needs it.

The school's principal, Jess Hutchinson, calls Craft a "resource," although both are quick to point out that the entire faculty exchanges ideas and tips about using technology. Craft has a classroom with tables along the perimeter, as well as a number high-definition screens along the walls, onto which he can project images.

"We are not one-to-one [one computer for each student] in our school yet; we're bound by what the district's plan is, but it is coming. We have very rapidly come out of the 'overhead and chalkboard age.' Our teachers went very quickly into smart boards and projectors. We have a number of teachers using iPads and netbooks . . . the faculty here is very hungry for it, and we absolutely encourage that," explains Principal Hutchinson.

The school has begun allowing students to bring their own devices to school, including laptops and smartphones. "Chris does not have one-to-one; we do, however, have iPad carts. He's adequately supplied with laptops and PCs," notes Hutchinson.

When considering decisions about what technology to pursue in a unit or lesson, Craft says, "What I'm looking at is, what I think it's going to be possible for them [students] to learn with these tools. And then, also, what I think I'm capable of learning about, in a reasonable amount of time, given that I can't know everything. And so the unit has got to have ample online resources, such as YouTube videos, and things like that."

MATCHING LEARNING GOALS AND TECHNOLOGY: STEM

Previously, Craft had a limited amount of time within which to work on a primary focus of Introduction to STEM: app-building. With the previous quarter system at CrossRoads, he had roughly nine weeks to move his class through the curriculum. But CrossRoads has changed to a semester system, and that has helped Craft expand his curriculum. Now, the first part of the semester is focused on app-building, and the second half is focused on engineering, with a student-interests-driven period of several weeks in between the two larger units.

Craft describes all of his classes as "inquiry-based and interest-driven." Previously, given the short terms, there was little whole-class instruction, and Craft organized the kids to work mainly in groups, in order to get them immediately oriented on the tasks at hand.

With more time, Craft can utilize, even more, a theory of learning he likes, based upon the work of the academic Richard Clark, who taught at the University of Southern California. Clark espoused a theory of "guided experiential learning," or GEL (pronounced "jell"). He uses this theory to introduce the technology that students will use, and then to help them use the technology to perform activities within the app-building lesson. Craft also follows other researchers who have worked in this area, such as David Kolb, a progenitor of experiential learning theory.

"Guidance in experience is absolutely critical; in order to apply this you have to know the goal at the end. It's very much skills-based. What is it I want my kids to understand when they leave my class? I want them to understand, first, the elements of a good app, and second, I want them to understand their own thinking process, when they download the app and use it, or delete it. They need to understand the design process, the icons. But it's undergirded by really good questions," comments Craft.

"In classes like mine I often observe that the focus seems to be on the 'experience' of the technology, whether that experience is guided or unguided," Craft remarks. "Purely unguided experience is problematic, as it's rooted in David A. Kolb's Experiential Learning Theory. The idea of unguided experience is, 'Let's give learners something to try without any context or previous experience.' After trying and presumably failing for lack of experience, the student is then taught. Learning is essentially a process of re-learning."

"Unguided experience can be good if there's prior knowledge and existing cognitive schemata. Where it's troubling is when there is a lack of experience. Without context or prior experience, learners often learn wrong information from their experimentation. This then has to be un-learned and re-learned. To mitigate this, I strive to learn with my kids when we reach a topic that is beyond my knowledge and theirs. That way I can help steer them down the right path because I presumably have more context and existing schema for any task," he comments.

"So what I try to do is work through guided experiential learning," adds Craft. This means, breaking down a lesson, such as app building, into chunks, discussing it first, then modeling or demonstrating some piece of it—such as how to embed a picture in a document online—and then letting students try to do the same thing.

Typically, when students first come into Craft's class, they are seated at their tables along the wall, and they then all come together to converse as a group at the two large tables, moved together, in the center of the room—the so-called Harkness Tables, after the learning method pioneered at Phillips Exeter Academy and named for a school donor. The original method focused on students engaged in a Socratic-style discussion with a teacher around a table. During a conversation at the Harkness Tables about the lesson, Craft may project images on to the screens around the room. Once that conversation is completed, students can return to their tables and begin working on computers and with their small groups.

As Craft describes it, "When we start out, the sixth graders are not on the computers. First they have to watch me; after we come to Harkness, we have a conversation, and they have to listen to what other children are saying around a big old table. I drive the bus, and run the demonstration for a little while. We have 'Come to Harkness' time. There's movement, then I say, 'Grab your computers,' and then they are logging in."

Besides laptop screens, "there are eight high-definition screens for them to look at, at each table" along the sides of the room, "so each group of students is never more than a few feet away from a screen, even when they are around the Harkness Table."

Explains Craft: "My goal is to provide information in their line of sight as much as possible. This helps make the technology itself invisible and more transparent. Much like when someone installs a new window in a home, no one looks at the window, they look at what is beyond. By providing multiple places for students to look, I find that it becomes more natural, and they look not at the screen but rather at the content displayed."

To further illustrate, he says, "We're having a conversation. We recently spent a lot of time talking about Google Glass—stuff that interests kids. Usually our class period starts with a conversation about some really good questions, then I'll express what they really need to understand. GEL is principally skill-based, and so there are good questions, and then there's demonstration. 'Now you think about what you want to build, now let's talk about how we will build what you are thinking about.' It gets more complex each time; running concurrently with that skills development is idea development."

When it comes to app building, "We're looking at a design characteristic, and UI [as a user-interface characteristic], in looking at a desired outcome. A student will say, 'I'm not someone who will use this tool.' I'll say, 'Let's see what is the best fit for you.'" In Craft's classes, students have built apps to capture the progress of soccer teams, like South Carolina United Football Club; the work of a local dance academy; and the world of *Little House on the Prairie*, the Laura Ingalls Wilder book, which was adapted for television.

With the shorter terms, Craft had used a variety of technology, from Raspberry Pi and Arduino to Genuitec's MobiOne Web-app-building software—along with some paper—to help his students in building apps. However, with semester-length classes dawning, Craft searched out new app-building tools online. One he likes is called AppShed, available at appshed.com, which he found after some searching, and talking to online colleagues.

He continues conversations to elicit student interests. "'Let's talk through the apps that you use more often; what do you like about them, what is it we can extrapolate from the app that we use?' Then we turn that around and use that as our exploration. Students learn 'successful apps fill a need that I didn't know I had,' and then how are we going to go forward and fill one of those needs? How will we actually develop that?"

"App building was initially nine weeks, and it's a very complicated process for sixth graders—navigating something like app development. This past summer, I found a tool that makes it more accessible for middle school students. I'm dealing with sixth graders, and app building is difficult. Plus, I have a semester, instead of just nine weeks, to work on this with them. So last year we just dove right in. But, since I knew that I would have more time, and I knew that I would move through it at a greater pace, with more context, we start off with all the technology resources that are available to them in the sixth grade. We familiarize ourselves with the computer, login, the browsers, the Google apps. 'You've got to do this if you want to search.' It's important because I distribute all of my documents through Google Docs. So I show them, here's how you use it. But it's more than that. It's 'GEL,' with some independent inquiry time, as well. So the steps are: here's the tools, here's the Google Docs, now you try it."

For example, says Craft: "I create a document, I live-share it with the group, because I have a group with all their [school] e-mail addresses, so I'm able to share it with them in two clicks. They [the students] are able to see their names pop up" next to the document, online, in Google Docs.

Craft uses a free programming script called gClassFolders, which Craft says is not that easy to use. It involves putting shared documents in an online folder, and "it allows automatic sharing between me and that student," and "in that way I use that folder to auto-distribute documents." He notes there is also a paid sharing solution, called Hapara, which also works with the Google apps.

To monitor students, Craft uses a feature "within AppShed; I can see their progress." But he also notes that via his iPad, or "my computer, I can also see their screens, so anyone that is off-task, or taking a little too long spending time picking out icons for their app, I'll be able to tell."

The last unit in the semester is robotics. For a robotics platform, Craft used kits created by LEGO Education, because he had worked with the materials in the kits as part of a LEGO Robotics afterschool club he has run. "That one is one of the more accessible platforms for kids," Craft explained, noting there is a color-coded process that helps students make progress.

"It's a series of challenges, and then I do the teaching, and then I get out of the way. So, they figure out the [successive] challenges, and at the end they are building and programming reasonably complex robots," recalls Craft, who has recorded video of the finished robots moving around the classroom.

MATCHING LEARNING GOALS AND TECHNOLOGY: WORLD LANGUAGES

Craft taught world languages—a precursor to later choices by students in choosing one foreign language to learn—through the end of the 2012–2013 school year. His attention to differentiation, and to integrating technology in a sensible way, is evident in his discussion of that time.

"Basically," said Craft, through technology and good teaching techniques, he sought to have the students "see it [the language] and interact with the vocabulary," through an e-learning system, like Haiku, "to really give them a chance to interact with certain vocabularies."

Still, much of what Craft does is independent of any technology choices. He's focused on encouraging critical thinking, and notes that when students are working on their writing, he is clear about what they need to focus on in turn—whether online or not. "I want my class to support the Common Core standards for writing argumentatively, so 'justify your choice'" when you write a essay, he counsels his charges.

He says that he initially found some of the existing curricula to be "a mile wide and an inch deep," and was concerned that it did not foster meaningful learning or provide the kind of foundation that would be useful when students would choose to study one language with greater intensity. At least a partial solution, in his mind, was to make sure that he reached out to as many resources as possible, whether through the Internet, or via different mediums, to bring in a variety of resources—and resources that would connect with kids in ways that were individual to their learning styles.

"We didn't get into grammar; it [the course] gets kids to be exposed to taking one of the four languages," Craft observed. "It is my opinion that for vocabulary to hit, and to enact changes in long-term memory, kids need to hear and interact with the language lots and lots of times." So for Craft and his students, that meant Craft put words on the screen for them to see, to hear them both from his voice and from audio recordings, to say the words to themselves and other students, to put the words down on paper in their notes, and then to let them see it in an online quiz.

DIFFERENTIATING

Craft likes the idea of groups working together on application building, as it allows for differentiation based on their interests. For Craft, the entire lesson over many weeks is an exercise in critical thinking skills. It's a process that examines a number of areas of thought: the scientific method, experimentation, invention, product engineering, and business.

"Different groups are at different levels of readiness. The students will often be ambitious: 'We want to create, and to make the next *Angry Birds* [a video game app].' The first steps are generally to build on something that exists, however. It's creativity with constraints. When we have constraints to our creativity, we are more creative. We also review the app store policies," Craft notes.

Differentiation extends to different types of media—even traditional ones. Although Craft runs a largely paperless classroom, he is mindful of student preferences, and for that reason does not ban paper outright. "My definition of paperless is: I'm not giving handouts. I don't want to force them to take notes in an impersonal way. 'Paperless' should never be shoved down their throats. There are some kids who are going to be distracted with a computer in front of them, or not quick to type on them, and so they can have a notebook in front of them. It's all about efficiency. Sometimes you need to grab a sticky note and stick it to the side of your computer," says Craft.

The idea is that he will try not to make copies and increase the flow of paper going to students.

Another opportunity for differentiation occurs in the period between the two main units. When it comes to this buffer period between application building and engineering—a period of several weeks—he draws out student interests to guide learning. He has worked on a design

challenge with the kids that can be found at marshmallowchallenge
.com, and provides a fun introduction to engineering.

"I ask, 'What would you like to learn, what interests you?,' and I
get back all kinds of great responses from the kids." Craft's students expressed interests in NASA's technology for space exploration and other
kinds of space technology, in law enforcement technology, and in drones
of various kinds. After reaching out to experts in these fields via e-mail,
Web sites, and social media, Craft was able to round up appearances by
some of them in person, or via a video link.

For NASA, the class conducted a Webinar with NASA scientists after
registering online for a time on the NASA Digital Learning Network.
Separately, for a discussion about modern space suits, a professor at the
Massachusetts Institute of Technology, Dava Newman, spoke with the
class via video about her work in this field. Other experts—from the
FBI, from Embry-Riddle Aeronautical University—also spoke with, and
to, the class.

For the video links, Craft used videoconferencing software, and also
Google's Hangout application. He requested, and received, permission
to record some of the appearances; he then was able to upload recorded
material to his Google drive as a "private, unlisted file" and shared it
with his students via their e-mail addresses. Although viewing it uses
Google's YouTube player, the file is not accessible on the public portion
of YouTube, Craft says. He notes that he can also embed the video in a
secure Google site.

NETWORKING

Hutchinson, the principal, observes to me, "Chris is incredibly proficient; I often go to him myself for advice. For example, 'What do you
think about this software?' My task is to recognize where my technology
leaders are in the building and put them to use."

He can also help share information among teachers. And while
Hutchinson calls Craft a "resource" for him and others, Craft believes

the key to successful technology integration at CrossRoads is constant sharing of information among all of the school's professionals.

For Hutchinson, successful technology integration at CrossRoads means bringing people and resources together. "Part of that is just being mindful of my daily conversations in the hallways with teachers, being mindful of the language that is supportive of those ideas. Permission is there to explore these new instructional strategies. I end up facilitating conversations between teachers. It's very important, because they learn from each other . . . We don't want these folks living on an island. My role is . . . helping to facilitate that collaboration in the schools, and setting the culture that supports it."

At school, some teachers are trying out platforms like Edmodo. "That's definitely some technology that our teachers have really started to use a good bit, students can go home and stay connected with their teacher, sitting on their couch, using their device; it's gotten very user-friendly. There are different levels of success with that," comments Hutchinson.

Inevitably, the technology at school does not always work properly. "Some aren't comfortable working through these issues, some are all over it. We have great tech support in our district. It's great when it's working, and you have a great lesson plan, and then the server goes down, or issues similar to that. Teachers have to be prepared; it's always an issue with technology. It's awesome when it works, and when it's not it can be a struggle for a teacher."

"Our teachers absolutely want to learn and implement these strategies, using technology, but there is also the issue of time, and finding time to learn, and it's my job to help make that time available," says Hutchinson. "We try to keep updated through e-mail, and we try to give them opportunities to, for instance, check out this link. Our teachers do blog, and we ask them to share instructional strategies through that blog. Checking out the blog . . . that's been a way to facilitate some growth. Setting a culture, in the school, in modeling the use of technology from administrators. It helps everyone feel comfortable about taking risks, and trying things in the classrooms. They need to talk to each other and communicate," he adds.

Craft explains, "There's a groundswell effort within the faculty to use technology, and learn about it. Sometimes I'll sit down and talk with them, but it's a real self-starting crew at our school. Our teachers have a really strong culture of innovation that supports moving beyond the status quo, and we have common planning among the departments, too, and the departments are talking to each other." He notes that departmental meetings are also a good place to exchange experiences with, and discoveries about, technology.

FOSTERING DIGITAL LITERACY

With the help of Craft and other CrossRoads teachers, students learn to become more digitally literate. They work on the issues related to obtaining, manipulating, and archiving resources they need, and the work they produce, online. And they manage working on their own devices under a "bring your own device" program (BYOD); these might include smartphones, tablets, or laptops. Students also learn how to properly credit sources, whether they are producing work online or not.

"BYOD has been more difficult than anticipated. They are sixth graders, after all, and they have not yet been taught the appropriate use of these devices for learning; their devices have been for play. It's tempting to say that they have grown up with it, and so they'll figure it out. The truth is that they need someone to guide them. I say, 'Let's talk about this powerful device.' I try to model that. I'm not a hundred percent. I'll hit up the Google apps . . ." with students expressing surprise at the range of functions available via the apps.

Hutchinson agrees, noting "there was a little bit of growing pain; there was a shift in mindset that needed to happen . . . It's OK for a kid to pull that smartphone out and use it for instruction. But there's a lot that comes with that, such as having conversations with kids about responsible use. Fifty years ago, they had to monitor kids to keep kids from passing notes; nothing has really changed."

This comes up in the app-building unit, as he works with his students through cloud-based document sharing, such as Google Docs. "And that's the paradigm shift that they have to get them through. In elementary school, it's MS Word; there is just one Word document, and they save it to their flash drive. I have to get them beyond that mentality. 'You can edit through Web browsers; it's ubiquitously available, and you can edit it with another student.' It forms the foundation for everything in the semester. This is how I'm paperless, because I distribute everything to them through Google," says Craft.

"When a novice does something they've never done before, they will mess it up, and it's very arduous for them to unlearn what they've messed up; hence guided experiential learning is important. We say, 'Let's take it in smaller chunks.' I don't have to develop an entire lesson based on technology, just a small part, and it gives them a foundation. For instance, teaching them how to use Google Docs effectively, or using the Internet as a research tool. That's the only chunk we did today. That's plenty, for now. Or taking a document and then, 'OK, let's insert a map' into this. With guided experiential learning, they master things step by step. 'Once we get our minds wrapped around Google Docs, then we're going to start using Google Docs.' And then the learning starts to take place," says Craft.

ASSESSING

"STEM is career technical education to some extent," says Craft. "I frame it like this is their job; just come in every day and work. They are evaluated on certain metrics. Little seminars and a standard rubric. I go meet with group number 1; we'll sit down, do an annual review. How do we feel our progress has been? Each student has a binder. I want them to feel like a project manager in a creative field. Parents can see a copy of that rubric."

"The system allows me to generate a couple of reports," he notes. "I can print out what my formal grading has to say, but I can also print out what one particular child's grading is doing, to see a causal link between performance and the work."

For world languages, one innovation Craft believes has made some difference in the value of assessment to his students and their learning is the use of certain forms of student response devices—the "clickers" or "e-clickers." As Craft tells it, "In years past, as I was reviewing, I did a traditional review in whole class. Its reliance on raised hands from one or two kids" posed problems. "As a student myself, I dreaded being called on. I didn't want that spotlight or attention. I was a very introverted kid."

"The clickers allow every kid to participate. But there's a modicum of anonymity. There, on the board, the answer is revealed only by clicker number. Every kid does participate, and they are able to self-assess. They make a little note about how they did. Some kids do well. Through Google apps, projected on the screen by remote number, they get to see their results through remote software. There's an aggregate score, and each question has a point value. They get to see how they did, and how the class did. They are repetitively and cognitively interacting with that content."

Beyond this, Craft says he used a traditional grading structure in world languages, such as quizzes, tests, and classwork.

"In STEM class last year, because of the short time, it was a project-based grade. This year, because we've got some chance to do introductory learning, there is minor classwork grading. Half their grade is daily classwork, quizzes, and the other half are project scores. It's a little more holistic, because it's looking at it as if it's their job, and then, this is their job performance evaluation," explains Craft.

REFLECTING

For Craft, the technology is secondary to his relationship with his students. He recalls his own student days, saying, "Some of the best teachers I had knew me personally, teachers that I still keep in touch with today. The reason that school buildings are still valuable is because of the relationship and expertise that can be found with the teacher. It's where students get to interact with teachers and students, and start from somewhere."

It's for this reason that Craft's advice to teachers who are integrating technology is equal parts psychosocial and technocratic. "As you're getting to know your kids, be thinking through what types of learning will directly connect with those kids, and at the same time, ways to become more efficient," counsels Craft.

For teachers who want to integrate more technology, "I would say, let's take a baby step to be more efficient. For example, are you finding that you are grading too many papers? Let's address that, and use technology as an efficiency-increasing tool." Craft suggests finding ways to do online assessments that can be graded by the software, as some teachers now do with certain kinds of quizzes or progress checks that dump the results into a spreadsheet. He has set up his grading so that he can generate his own reports through Google apps that show student progress.

In general, "I use directed instruction and directed help. I say, 'Here are the resources you need," given the wide variety of student interests. I circulate with on-demand help and sometimes that is saying I have absolutely no idea what the answer is, so let's figure it out. I sometimes end up being the guy that just does the Googling," says Craft.

Of the shift in education toward project-based learning and technology integration, Craft says, "I don't know that I'm asking to carve out time to do high-level tech use, and I'm not saying that we should abandon all of the standards in favor of some communal, project-based learning environment. However, if we come to greater efficiencies through the use of tech, then we'll gain back the extra time we've spent developing PBL-type curricula."

"It's never about the technology, it's about the learning," Craft comments, describing his orientation toward his practice. "The more efficient we teachers can be, the more we can focus on kids and custom-tailoring the learning to our kids."

7

"I Want Them to Be Uploaders"

Joshua Silver

NINTH TO TWELFTH GRADE
ENGLISH LANGUAGE ARTS
Arrowhead Park Early College High School,
Las Cruces, New Mexico

Given his philosophy of fearless experimentation with technology, it is perhaps not surprising that English teacher Josh Silver is teaching himself to play guitar using GarageBand software for iPad—nor that Silver has racked up a number of awards for his teaching. In 2012, The College Board named Silver the Southwest Region recipient of its Bob Costas Grants for the Teaching of Writing. That year, the New Mexico Society for Technology in Education also tapped Silver as Outstanding Teacher of the Year. The following year, the Las Cruces Public Schools Foundation named Silver its Teacher of the Year. And, along with a team of teachers, Silver has assisted his school in winning thousands of dollars in hardware through a corporate-sponsored contest.

Among other things, the awards cite his ability to engage students using technology. For Silver, that describes a large range of activities for his students, two-thirds of whom will be the first of their family to go to college, echoing the mandate of Arrowhead Park Early College High School (APECHS), a three-year-old school on the New Mexico State University (NMSU) campus.

"I'm really interested in how students communicate and collabo-
rate," explains Silver. "I don't want them to be downloaders. I want
them to be uploaders, which requires them to produce something, and
that product is something to share with other people. I bear the respon-
sibility of kids to be uploaders of good information for other people."

Silver became APECHS Dean of Students in the fall of 2013. He
continues to teach students in a yearbook class, and also teaches, and
facilitates teacher training, at New Mexico's virtual public school, In-
novative Digital Education and e-Learning (IDEAL). Additionally,
he teaches several different courses to NMSU students in that school's
teacher credential program.

RAMPING UP

APECHS opened to 117 students in 2011. It now serves several times
that number. Honoring its imperative to see that all of its students graduate, and then enter college or university, students are all dual-enrolled
in NMSU; technically, they are dual-enrolled at Doña Ana Community
College, which is also on the NMSU campus. Students may end up going
to a different school, but they work above grade level during their time
at the school. Thus, freshmen typically work on ninth- and tenth-grade
English, while sophomores work on eleventh- and twelfth-grade material. Students who stay on track then work on associate's degree–level
English in eleventh and twelfth grade. Those students can enter NMSU
as juniors, saving them time and money.

There are exceptions, where students need extra time to "reinforce skills," and Silver has taught a sophomore class that is taking the
eleventh-grade material at a slower pace, using "tech to enhance learning and deepen the curricular experience."

Students have complete access to the university library, and they
also have a login for the university that is separate from their APECHS
login. And while teachers can access YouTube at school, students, as
minors, cannot access it. This has caused some organizational and technical hiccups for teachers, as they try to manage the different logins and

passwords students need for both enrollments, notes Silver, who adds that the benefits of this setup outweigh the challenges it can bring.

Students can bring their own devices to APECHS, even as they have the ability to check out a laptop as part of a class set that Silver has. He also has multiple smart boards and video cameras. APECHS principal Jennifer Amis notes that the district's superintendent was determined to build a technology-centric school: the Internet connections within the school are "very, very reliable," she says.

Explains Amis, "We want the students to be able to hear a lecture, see a lecture, replay the lecture. Part of the strategy is to provide 24/7 access to their instruction." To achieve this, compromises were made in conceptualizing the school; for example, it does not have competitive athletics or performing arts.

"We don't have a one-to-one initiative," Amis continues, "but teachers have iPads, they have laptops and Chrome books. Students are able to check those out. And students also are able to bring their own devices and use those. When they are within our classrooms, they are subject to the Internet protection laws that we are subject to," says Amis.

More hardware came the school's way in 2013, when Silver and two other teachers supervised and guided the school's student video entry in a Samsung-sponsored contest focused on using science, technology, engineering, and mathematics education to solve problems; the APECHS students designed a rainwater-collection system, and created a video to show how it would work in the community. Ultimately, the school won $100,000 worth of technology, including computers, smart boards, and LED TVs. Silver's piece of this project involved guiding students in the scriptwriting, and reviewing the narrative.

TEACHING DIGITAL LITERACY

Realia, or real-world examples of text—such as newspapers or comment threads for a book published on Amazon or iTunes—is material that Silver likes to draw upon in order to provide perspective on, if not actual lessons in, digital literacy. This might involve pulling up the online comments about a high school mainstay, such as a widely read classic like F. Scott Fitzgerald's *The Great Gatsby*, or something as mundane as the reviews of a local restaurant. It also helps break down common forms of communication into manageable chunks.

"It's not been an explicit lesson as much as it's been a tool. It's never been the end result—it's teaching literacy about when that tool [research using individuals' online comments] is appropriate, and what does 'appropriate' mean," he says.

That said, Silver comments, "It's really a very relevant consumer lesson to look at [Web] sites like Yelp, or Urbanspoon, or Chowhound. It's amazing how much consumers rely on those things, and also how trusting the kids are of everything on the Internet. I'm always amazed that they assume whatever is on there is true, or right. It's often just an opinion," says Silver. "And it's that media literacy skill that I try to explore. It's a really nice way to ask, 'Does this person have a certain agenda, does this person have a certain P.O.V. [point of view]?' They probably have a different view if they have expertise in the area in question, than if they do not have expertise."

What he is hoping to develop in his students, moreover, is a sense of what constitutes evidence for something: for an assertion, a statement, a belief. This theme of discernment with regard to evidence crops up often in discussion with Silver about his work; he is interested in his students' understanding what facts and motivations drive others' writings—whether that writing is in the form of a book or an online brochure.

"This kind of activity explores audience, and purpose, and speaker, and this stream of information on any Web site, which you have to know how to sort through, and to see what is valuable to you," he notes. "I love sites that rely on reviews from users because it's this great way to study credibility. Students may not understand that topic in nonfiction, but can surely 'get it' on Yelp. So we will pick a favorite place on Yelp, often a local restaurant, and read the reviews. There are always great ones and always bad ones. So we read and inevitably, the kids disagree. Then, that opens the conversation to talk about evidence."

He has templates for Yelp-style reviews that he posts on his Blackboard page, which students can use. "It might ask, 'What experience did you have that makes you feel that way?' The kids have to support their ideas with evidence. We often do a Yelp review over a [*Great*] *Gatsby* party, and this makes the kids use evidence to support their ideas. I think reviews are a great way for kids to understand that we all come from a perspective. Another example: if a librarian gives a book five stars, and a college student, with an Amazon profile pic of him doing a keg stand, gives it a 'one' and calls it the worst book ever, we have a clearer understanding of point of view, in both cases."

Silver reflects that he may not yet have developed the best lesson to explore this area, but it's an evolving area of exploration for his pedagogy for kids' online conversations. "I don't know that I do that very well, but it's a life skill, to be able to discern what is legitimate, and what is not, in this context."

He recalls that at some point he was looking for a current news example, and students found a Twitter hashtag related to the 2012 Newtown, Connecticut, school shootings; he used this to look at language. Speaking of using social media, in general, he said, "I want them to see the emerging tools as an integrated part of learning. I want them to know how to responsibly use what they have."

MATCHING LEARNING GOALS AND TECHNOLOGY

Until his job change, Silver had been teaching junior-level English to freshman, and senior-level English to sophomores—a majority of whom will be the first in their family to go to college or university. He has also taught Advanced Placement English.

His signal philosophy is to put models, and examples, of writing and communication in a variety of media out to the students—in any way possible. "I think the kids just really need to see a lot of examples. I try to use any tech platform to provide a space to see a lot of these. By the time we've put a product up there, it's gone through a lot of individual and group work. I want them to see what creates good work."

From search to Twitter to online editing to blogging, Silver then assists students in producing that "good work" themselves. It might be a public service announcement, an instruction manual, or a critical analysis of literature or a dramatic work. Often, the work of learning in his class involves his students working with him to create the rubric they will use in evaluating their work.

Silver's pedagogy is also often marked by breaking down barriers, and one that is common in high schools is among separate class periods of the same subject matter. In addressing this, an activity that Silver likes is to open discussions between, and among, not just students of one class, but students of multiple sections of the same class. "Once it's on the discussion board, then we discuss what's exemplary about these examples. That's a pretty common pattern for us in class. The examples are also turned into the discussion board, just so that everyone can see them."

He explains further: "Since I taught the same class [English 11] multiple times each day, it was easy for me to use online discussion boards across all sections of the class. For example, I would pose a question, such as 'What does it mean to live with integrity?,' on the board, and have all sections answer on the same board. Then when we came back to that in class, I had the contributions of all of my students, not just from that single class. It also allowed us the chance to edit work and read lots of examples when doing an assignment. Again, if they had an analysis essay to submit for peer edit, I'd usually have them turn it in on the discussion board so that all students in all sections could read and edit. Then we may spend one or two class days just working individually reading the work of students. It just gave us a larger library of 'stuff' to draw from."

Silver's curriculum draws from many sources, while addressing multiple standards. It involves the learning of formal language use—in some cases, by contrasting that language with the informal language of everyday casual conversation, as in tweets and cell phone texts. Often students are asked to make presentations, using either a slide show or video format. They do this when they create public service announcements, which examine the idea of influencing public opinion through communication.

In his freshman class, students read Arthur Miller's 1949 Nobel Prize–winning drama *Death of a Salesman*—now a high school staple. "I am a fan of having kids study and understand trends. We do lots of timelines for this reason, as well. With *Death of a Salesman* it's this great time to study sales, and what Willy Loman does for a profession," Silver comments. Silver also uses *Salesman* as a launching pad for wider inquiry into advertising and trends of the play's immediate post–World War Two era.

To organize an exploration of the context of the play, Silver obtains lots of copies of commercials from the Internet. Using an application like KeepVid.com, he drags the files into iTunes, then syncs them on to all of the class iPads. That allows him to start an online discussion that his students can join, using his outline regarding trends or period influences that can be discerned in a given commercial. Or they can judge the commercials based on standard appeals to character, beliefs, social cachet, and utility.

"Once there, the kids all have individual access to them, and can view [them] as often as they want," explains Silver. "I like this. It becomes very individualized. Lots of teachers, I bet, are watching commercials to help kids understand audience and message, and ethos, logos, and pathos. The difference here is that I don't have to lead the discussion. They all have the content and can watch their way, and then I can go around and discuss individually with kids."

In the past, Silver has asked students to create a presentation on the online poster-creation Web site Glogster. "Yes, there is a board conversation. That is usually a discussion about which [element]—logos, ethos, or pathos—is the strongest in advertising, and why. And then I want the students to find print examples (mostly just 'cause posting video is too difficult) of an ad that uses the one they think was the least important," Silver wrote in an e-mail. "The presentation is graded on a rubric that we make as a class. I make just about all of the rubrics with the class. I think it's helpful for them to all understand what is expected."

Students execute an extended Internet research project looking into political and social influences of the 1950s, then posting about those, and developing essays, which they peer-edit online; or they can act out a scene and then film it and post it to the class page. This unit also examines advertising of that era using the Aristotelian persuasive analysis focused upon *logos*, *ethos*, and *pathos*—appeals to such things as social status and utility of a given product or service.

"The goal of this unit is to understand the concept of influence," says Silver, "and to understand the power of words to influence. We do this by creating our own public service announcements," noting that it's the work that goes into planning and preparing the announcements that he's interested, in as much as the final result.

From his perspective, there are two overarching phases to this. First, Silver models on his smart board—and his students research online, and post online, and discuss—the differences between informal and formal styles of communication. With the first phase, "we spend a lot of time first looking at the truth campaign, http://www.thetruth.com /about/, and then talk about messages and how to best deliver them." During this phase, "the way I will organize it first, I will put examples [of PSAs] on the iPads, and that is one of the best ways to get what I want, is to give them lots of good examples." The students can view these repeatedly: "It gives them a lot of buy-in; you can guide the conversation to get what you want in the rubric, then give them an end deadline."

Second, the writing of the announcement is itself broken down into phases. Within the early writing phase, students are identifying the target audience, along with the message and purpose of the announcement. Students are also asked to write reflections on what language they are using for their production, and why they chose that style of language. Once scripts are prepared, then students can work on camera angles and shots, and what they are embedding into their announcement.

"Especially with the second one [second phase], it's really important to have those production scripts: preparing it, doing it, and reflecting on that. I really like to break things up that way. I like it because the technology piece comes into play when I want it to, in order not to have the technology drive the lesson. I want it to be the vehicle of it, not the focus of the lesson, and breaking down the writing process helps that," notes Silver.

Silver gives them a due date when presentations will be made, and asks them to post their progress on the class's Blackboard site, via Google Docs, or by sending e-mail to Silver himself. "I don't want to manage a bunch of mini-deadlines," he says.

"I like that we're not all doing the same thing; I want to give the kids the expectation that 'here is the due date' and post your progress," explains Silver. "If I can jump in and see what they are doing, then that's fine."

Comments Silver, "That, to me, is how to look at kids' learning: I'm really interested in their preproduction, when they are creating their own public service announcements . . . and their ability to apply various techniques. For example, 'This is our target audience, and so I'm going to use that particular technique or that influence.' The technology only comes into play after they have a really clear idea of what they are doing."

He asks them to plunge into *Macbeth* in another unit. With *Macbeth*, the character is the thing. As such, students may create a mock-Facebook page for a character. As Silver tells it, he just asks them to transpose what they know of a character into a Facebook-like profile—for which purpose there are many templates online. "There are lots [of Facebook-like templates online]; the one I usually use is a [Power-Point] file. Then they have to make this. I love this because it's a format they know, but it also requires students to think about their character's interactions with other characters, their basic bio info and more. It's really layered," he elucidates.

Breaking it down, Silver says, "I assign the students a character from the play. Then we all use the same Facebook[-like] template. I don't want kids copying each other's, so in Blackboard, you can set up a discussion board so that a student cannot see the work on the discussion board in the other threads, until he or she submits on that board. That way, they can't see anyone else's until they have turned theirs in. I use this a lot."

"After we have done the reading . . . we do a lot of talk about the characters and point of view. Facebook is great [as a model] because we can talk about public image as well as friends and context. And timelines. So we do this offline through a PowerPoint template. The students pick up the template through Blackboard and then create the page. They do the photos and have to create wall posts from friends . . . Then we print them, and share them," Silver further explains.

Of his curriculum, Silver observes in an e-mail, "There are still some days where I want the kids to do a very traditional . . . [read: boring] lesson. But there are reasons for me choosing that. Maybe I feel they need to practice with short answer questions and using evidence in their writing. But other times, I heavily rely on tech to deliver the message. It's not even like an integration as much as just a way of doing things in class. It's as essential to me as pencil and paper. And now, it's probably more essential than pencil and paper. We don't use those too much."

FOSTERING COLLABORATION AND COMMUNICATION

Collaboration and communication—between individual students as well as between students and the world—are overarching themes of Silver's teaching: bringing groups together in class to create something, working through it using document sharing, and then posting it online for the entire class to see. Shifting learning, and accountability for that learning, to the student, is an outgrowth of this philosophy, he says. Silver mixes online work with paper work, printing out some directions while asking students to do some work online.

"One of the ways we've done that is the analysis of pretty nontraditional text—for example, a group working to evaluate the readability of an instruction manual. These are texts that are not traditional ELA [English language arts] texts. They work together on, say, an instruction manual for putting together a table, and they discuss how that explanation could be improved in writing," explains Silver.

"Collaboration is a great way for them to practice skills in a 'safe' environment. That's my goal. They also are able to learn from each other. With that group, as with all groups, they don't need just one teacher. Setting up my class like this gives them lots of teachers."

One example of collaboration is creating their own instruction manual, which Silver sees as a ubiquitous example of standard text; creating one also gives students a chance to teach others how to do something by communicating clearly and directly. After looking at many of these individually, the class begins to work on their own manuals in groups, but with an eye toward having individual voices become distinctive within the manual. The class discussion begins by addressing what students think makes a good instruction manual; Silver can then post some these ideas online. Silver will have students find versions of both "good" and "bad" instruction manuals online, so that they have a sense of how they want their final manual to look, sound, and read. Together, they build a rubric for the unit.

"The 'good example piece' is very powerful, and the rubric is nice to have, and hopefully they use it, but especially when they can compare those to the original instruction manual," says Silver. "So, in this case . . . they'll be working in a group of four that's very much rubric-based. There are some tasks that are individual, some are group. The reason I move them back and forth is to hold them all individually accountable; what they're creating is usually a Google doc that is downloaded and saved as a PDF, and then I have them upload that to Blackboard" for more class discussion.

"We might look at instruction manuals for ceiling fans, say, which often have good instruction manuals. Another time, it was a big set of unassembled chairs. What I usually have them do is come up with a set of questions, which respond to how these could be improved, and then also what was exemplary about the text. I'll usually have them create a Google doc as a group, or a Blackboard wiki. Then they're back on their own, but working collectively on this document. I want them to have four distinctive voices in the document. That turns into an individual manual, later on. In the meantime, embedded in this are layout lessons, a publishing lesson. There are four contributors," explains Silver.

To set this up, "The first thing I did was print off a lot of instruction manuals for lots of different things. Ceiling fans, IKEA furniture, televisions, etc. As many instruction manuals as I could find. A quick Google search yields lots. Then we spent a day in class just looking at them in small groups and creating charts of what we liked and what we didn't about them. Some common patterns will (probably) emerge. They liked sequential steps that were numbered. They like BOTH diagrams and text. They liked having a Web site with video (as opposed to a phone number which they usually agree they will never call)," he says.

"Then we play board games," to get a better sense of reading and using good directions, he says. "I try to find ones that they have never played: Faux-Cabulary is the common one I use. They have to read the directions to learn how to play it. Then we talk about how that worked. They have to make up a new game with the same pieces from Faux-Cabulary. They have to write their directions out and share them with another group. This is a day."

"Finally, they then need to choose their product," for which they will write a manual. "This is up to them, but usually I make them choose an essential item from a current text we have read, or are reading. Up to them. Everyone has their own. And from this, they need to make their instruction manual . . . This then turns into a discussion about marketing and target audience, designing the box, etc. This probably takes us four days," he says.

With all this, Silver says he's a proponent of classic English Language Arts content. "I think it's important to note that my curriculum is often very traditional. In the eyes of many, probably too traditional. We read lots of classic literature, as I'd imagine many classes are doing. With that, though, I find ways to use the technology. So, my core curriculum hasn't really changed. What has, though, is the delivery method," he says.

NETWORKING AND PROFESSIONAL DEVELOPMENT

In some ways, Silver's professional development path works in reverse; rather than seeking out professional development as a student, he's gleaning ideas and reflecting upon his own teaching while instructing adults through two NMSU courses he teaches for pre-service credential candidates.

One course is a general seminar, partly administered online with some face-to-face meetings, that addresses issues arising in, specifically, secondary school instruction. The other course is a content-area reading course that explores the "relationship between literacy and all content areas" and "a variety of ideas that foster reading, writing, listening, and speaking." Given that NMSU is where Silver obtained his own credential, it is a comfortable setting within which to network, to prepare the new teachers, and to pursue his own learning.

"These courses keep me up-to-date on research. And they also challenge everything that I'm doing in class," remarks Silver. "I love when one of my college students asks me why I am doing something. I also learn a lot from the students and their new ideas. I love both classes because I am not just working with English teachers. Instead, I'm working with teachers of lots of different contents. It challenges me to think about how some of my ideas apply to kids in all subjects," he adds.

In between this and his APECHS duties, Silver continues to teach at IDEAL, the state's online school. There Silver has taught a range of English-related courses for secondary students, and there he continues to develop courses, train teachers, and lead personal learning communities for instructors.

Meanwhile, Silver attended the annual conference of the Association for Career and Technical Education in Las Vegas at the end of last year (2013). The conclave gave him some ideas to chew on regarding future APECHS curricula. "My interests in education are always evolving, and more and more I see the need for a strong career technical education program at the high school level—one that requires students to actively think about career and what skills must be attained in order to be successful in that career," says Silver, adding that a theme, such as medicine, may be explored at APECHS, with an expansion of career pathways through new courses or additional or altered curriculum.

PLANNING FOR THE FUTURE

Last school year began a new chapter in Silver's career, when he moved into the dean's slot. He's still teaching one class for students who are producing the yearbook. As a dean, Silver finds that he is able to affect student learning in ways somewhat different from those as an English teacher. Among those ways are advocating for students on a range of issues, communicating with parents, advising individual students about current and future academic plans, and building student schedules.

The new roles gives him "a stronger understanding of the whole student. I am increasingly interested in the many ways that a school can support students. From a tech point of view, since I assumed this role, I've finished our school Web page and created a text-messaging network for our school. So I see increased communication as critical and have engaged in solving that," he says.

He stays in touch with his teaching practice by helming the yearbook class, composed of tenth and eleventh graders. "This was really more of a need for the school, but the entire book is built online. I get to work with kids that already have the [Adobe] Photoshop and Illustrator skills. I enjoy it, and it's a great chance for me to keep working with students. For the future, I maybe see myself in an admin role, but definitely do not want to lose the contact with kids. That's the best part," Silver proffers.

His syllabus for the content-area reading course he teaches at NMSU makes clear that Silver believes teachers can learn as much from teaching a class as the students themselves learn in that same class. It begins with a quote from the late Brazilian educator and philosopher Paulo Freire: "Literacy knows no boundaries—it ebbs and flows across all experiences and content areas."

Following the quote, Silver writes, "Freire contends a teacher's learning 'lies in their seeking to become involved in their students' curiosity and in the paths and streams it takes them through.'"

8

Routines and Pathways for Learning

Lindsey Taylor

NINTH TO ELEVENTH GRADE
MATH AND SCIENCE, EXCEPTIONAL CHILDREN
Ashbrook High School, Gastonia, North Carolina

Everyone seems to agree: what's going on in Lindsey Taylor's technology-centric special education classes is extra-special.

Co-teaching on a daily basis with remote, subject-qualified teachers who complement Taylor's certification in teaching special-needs children, Taylor and her co-teachers have boosted test scores and course completion rates among her students far beyond anything seen before in her student cohorts. For her achievements in working in this environment, Taylor has been honored by administrators, and most recently by North Carolina's virtual public school organization, with whom she works to implement the curriculum.

At the administration's behest, Taylor has hosted and been observed by fellow teachers, as well as by visitors to the school district, near Charlotte, where they observe her teaching students with a range of disabilities, in a special-needs program called Occupational Course of Study (OCS). For the past two school years Taylor has taught each of her classes with remote teachers from the North Carolina Virtual

Public School (NCVPS). The NCVPS OCS Blended Learning Program was established to bring co-teaching support on a remote basis to classroom teachers, to offer special needs and exceptional schoolchildren more intensive, dedicated teaching and support with online content and hands-on activities.

Taylor, in the high school classroom, and her NCVPS co-teachers, working often from their homes, have fashioned a curriculum and pedagogy that has Taylor's small groups of students passing high-stakes state-mandated subject exit exams, sometimes at a higher rate than their mainstream counterparts. Highly regarded by her school administration and digital co-teachers, Taylor was named NCVPS OCS 2013 Partner Teacher of Excellence. Taylor also recently finished work on a state-level committee, which is developing an NCVPS OCS history class that will be taught in a similar way to her classes.

BY NECESSITY, THE CURRICULUM Taylor teaches involves creating digital paths among herself, her co-teachers working remotely from Taylor, and her students; these pathways are then governed by a set of rules for feedback, responses, and grading. What Taylor brings to her class is twenty years of experience teaching special education classes, for which she holds a state certification; she also obtained a master's degree in special education with a concentration in cross-categorical disabilities.

She is the physical face of instruction, managing the class and leading the lessons from a digital folder that she and her co-teachers populate with lessons, based upon the co-teachers' understanding of the subject matter and Taylor's understanding of the particular needs of her students. The co-teachers find online resources, and together lessons and assessments are planned, reviewed, revised, and honed, as Taylor and her co-teachers see what works, and what does not. Technically, the curriculum is a turnkey product, delivered by NCVPS and its co-teachers to Taylor's physical classroom. In practice, it seems that Taylor and her co-teachers work together to refine and shape the taught curriculum, and they seem to appreciate and enjoy this arrangement.

When her odyssey with remote co-teachers began three years ago, Taylor was bringing nearly two decades of experience to her decision making. And while she had questions about how such an arrangement would work, even with an array of technology available to her, she now believes strongly in this paradigm for her students, who may be autistic, or face other developmental or cognitive processing challenges. Prior to NCVPS, she taught special education students on their own; she would also help special education students in inclusion classes, and then, sometimes, bring them back to her own classroom for more instruction, or remediation.

Now, Taylor is in constant contact via e-mail, chat, and phone with her co-teachers, and they meet synchronously, in real time, via chat or phone, once per week. Taylor says that the routinized rituals of the class and the progression of lessons, which are kept in carefully sequenced online folders, keep students on track, while offering them a chance to exercise choice and creativity within the confines of a heavily planned curriculum. The students, for their part, says Taylor, understand how the virtual relationship between two teachers, and their relationship with the students—sometimes as few as eight in number—supports their learning. Their disabilities can range from mild intellectual impairments, such as autism, to more severe intellectual and physical impairments of various kinds, such as blindness and issues with mobility.

Taylor has come to enjoy working with a co-teacher, using the technology available to her, and gets satisfaction from seeing her students achieve. Although sharing some activities (such as grading), originating some of the lesson content, and providing feedback, Taylor believes she is actually in more control of her students' learning than she was before. She has lots of technology to facilitate her teaching; she has the regular support of, and camaraderie with, another teacher, who is trained in the content-area subject matter; and she maintains a lot of control over the classroom, the direction of the teaching, and the students' learning.

Even with this high-tech infrastructure, students use paper in many ways, and engage in tactile lab work in science. What this blend of online and in-person teaching offers is a solid foundation for students who need extra help navigating school, and their own learning. For all the rules, repetition, and routine, Taylor says she feels more optimistic about the futures of her special students than she has in her entire career.

RAMPING UP

Taylor works in what has been an Ashbrook computer lab, so every student has a desktop computer. That's critical for the program to work as it does. Every student in Taylor's classroom has a computer at his or her desk, and Taylor herself has a complement of computers and a smart board. It's a big change from the past, explains Taylor, noting that previously special education classes often took "leftover textbooks that nobody wants."

Now Taylor pursues integration of technology in the classroom, and the management of student learning, from two angles. One angle takes into account the needs of her students. For student management, she relies on the Individualized Education Plans (IEPs) of each student, communication with students' parents and guardians, and a combination of other teachers' and administrators' knowledge of those students, her own understanding of the students' abilities, and her years of experience in special-needs classrooms. The other angle addresses the co-management of those students' learning through Taylor's professional relationship with the co-teachers, who are "highly qualified" in the specific subject matter, as spelled out in the No Child Left Behind law.

To run this blended classroom, with two teachers, one of whom is remote to the class, virtually all of the lessons must be accessible online by all parties. Students have folders they access online on Blackboard, a common classroom technology platform; these folders have been pre-loaded with a variety of activities, games, and notes. The pre-loading is, in part, a product of a required once-per-week synchronous discussion—either via phone or online chat—between the two teachers. The remote co-teacher will flesh out the instructional units ahead of time, with a variety of activities, lessons, games, and quizzes, based upon those discussions. Taylor then chooses from a range of activities, based upon her knowledge of her class; she also conveys to each co-teacher her preferences, ideas, and requests for content, lesson structure, and activities.

Without knowing much more, it might be easy to think of Taylor as the server, and her co-teachers as the chefs, but that is a misapprehension, she notes. "You do have to do lesson planning. You have to tell the online teacher where you are, and plan out your lessons, but you do have someone who is a highly qualified teacher," explains Taylor, recalling her advice to another Ashbrook teacher who was considering the move to the same model of teaching. "She kept saying she didn't want to give up control of her classroom. I told her that the face-to-face teacher really runs it; the online teacher provides the curriculum. You tell them what [curriculum components] you need. They grade a lot of the students' work for you."

Taylor is generous with her praise of NCVPS. From Taylor's standpoint, "I think the online teacher is more responsible for the curriculum than I am. The course is developed by a development team, and then the classroom teacher plans the lessons with the online teacher using the available course. The online teacher can supplement the course with more or different material, depending on how the students are performing. The classroom teacher is also welcome to supplement the instruction, but I personally feel like the online teacher is the expert in the curriculum, since the online teacher is highly qualified in the subject area. My area of expertise as the classroom teacher, and being the special education teacher, is knowing how to modify or adjust the material or present it in different ways in order to teach it to the students."

One of the co-teachers is Deanna Lancaster, a math teacher. Working from another part of the state, Lancaster explains that the regimented and electronic nature of the relationship pays dividends in correctly calibrating the teaching to the children's needs. It also provides a lot of immediate feedback from two different styles of assessment: formative self-adaptive learning quizzes, in which the score is immediately calculated for the student, and work submitted by the student, which must be graded and returned with feedback within twenty-four hours.

"Google Docs and e-mail are vital to our partnership," explains Lancaster. "We also use Blackboard IM [instant messaging on the Blackboard platform], via synchronous chat. We're required to meet once a week synchronously, so we do talk weekly. I give access to my documents to Lindsey when I sit down to work. I'll look at my planning spreadsheet and make available my comments [on student work] as well as attachments and other resources."

"We talk during a set day and time to chat about the weekly plans, IEP modifications, student behaviors, etc.," says Lancaster. In turn, Lancaster also meets with fellow online NCVPS teachers: "The monthly meeting I have is a monthly eLC meeting [e-learning community, rather than a PLC]. My NCVPS online teaching peers and I meet as a cohort to discuss tidbits pertinent to our course, such as errors that need to be fixed [in software], sharing of best practices, and things like that. The meetings are led by our course leaders and instructional leaders."

In class, notes Taylor, "my teaching is much more structured using technology. The students have a clear understanding of the way my class runs, what is expected of them, and how we will proceed though the lessons and units. When my class begins, we start out as a whole group. No student is allowed to be on their desktop computer until given instructions to log in. We review the daily announcement together, and if there is an interactive game that day, we play the game together on the smart board. I use a smart board daily to show the students daily announcements from their online teachers. This might be a video or an interactive game. I review the material for the day on the smart board, go over instructions for assignments, and show any videos, with guided notes for the students to complete, before giving instructions for the class to log in and complete the required assignments listed on the board."

Students find the required assignments in folders online that cover the kinds of activities the curriculum prescribes. Lesson content is broken out in completion, remediation, and mastery assignments, which are found in the eponymous folders. "The completion assignments are more for practice, the remediation assignments are for remediation if the students did not 'get' the material the first time through, and the mastery assignments are meant to prove mastery of the material," Lancaster explains.

"My students use computers almost every day for something in their coursework," adds Taylor. "There are days when we do hands-on activities, and there may be a portion of the assignment that the students are then required to 'type in' and send to their online teachers."

During breaks, and at day's end, Taylor says, "I look over the upcoming lessons and try out anything myself that I have never used before in class. Any new sites that require a username and password, I create those before my students ever log in to them, to save time. If I allowed them to create their own usernames and passwords, it would take twice as long, before we were ready to begin the assignment."

One advantage to working with NCVPS is that materials and curricula are revised regularly. Instead of "leftover textbooks," Taylor reports that "now, we have the stuff that is constantly being revised; that says a lot for the program. My administrator begged me for all that biology stuff."

MATCHING LEARNING GOALS AND TECHNOLOGY

Whereas many teachers in mainstream classrooms are trying to crack the code for independent, project-based learning, with access to computers and the Internet to spur engagement and creativity, Taylor is to some extent using technology to do the opposite—keep her kids moving together, and at the same pace, while allowing them to work on their own in a controlled way, once a foundation for the lesson is established. Students have choices, but those choices are made within a tight framework managed by Taylor and her co-teacher.

That goes for all of the classes Taylor teaches: in fall, tenth-grade algebra 1a, ninth-grade applied science, and tenth-grade biology; in spring, ninth-grade introduction to mathematics, eleventh-grade financial management, and tenth-grade algebra 1b. For each of these classes, Taylor works with a different co-teacher provided by the NCVPS organization.

NCVPS creates course content using Universal Design for Learning (UDL) principles, so "we provide multiple means of representation of the material along with multiple means of engagement," wrote Lancaster, in an e-mail. "The videos are ideal for our students as a visual, and as a way to engage the students. If one student learns better by writing and reading the material, guided notes along with the video would be the way to go. If a student enjoys games or needs quick review along with immediate feedback, games and CYK [check your knowledge] quizzes would work well with that student."

Lancaster says the curriculum is designed to meet students "where they are."

"The students are not meant to complete all of the activities in each lesson. The co-teachers [i.e., Taylor] decide which activities will work best for their students based on their skill set," she adds. "We provide students with a Notes folder [online] that houses video notes, written guided notes, games that review vocabulary and major concepts for the lesson, and 'Check Your Knowledge' formative assessment quizzes; all of these things are designed to teach the content but reach the students wherever they are most likely to learn."

"Game-ification" is an important piece of the curriculum—these teachers say the use of online games as a teaching tool engages students, keeps them motivated, adds a dash of excitement to something that may seem dry or unconnected to their lives, and helps them feel successful when they "win" a game. Lancaster explains that the completion activities—sometimes a game, sometimes not—often ask the students to do something "hands-on" and turn in to the classroom teacher, or to play a game, and then send a screenshot of the score to the online teacher.

"Some classroom teachers use the formative CYK quizzes at the end of the lesson to prove mastery . . . This is not ideal. So, with all of these activities built into the course, the student has choices about how he/she can learn and prove mastery . . . with the guidance of the co-teachers, of course," writes Lancaster.

"I send Lindsey a unit outline at the beginning of each unit that highlights for her what is in each lesson for that unit. She goes through the outline and chooses which activities she believes will be most worthwhile for our students. I can make suggestions about which ones the students should do based on pacing, difficulty, creativity, and enjoyment, but she is the EC [exceptional child] expert at the end of the day, and I defer to her. Since the course is developed by an NCVPS course development team and not our teachers, we do not create much for the course unless our co-teachers ask us for extra resources," says Lancaster.

The remediation folder, ideally, would only be accessed if the classroom teacher realizes that she's exhausted her resources from the notes, completion activities, and mastery assignments folders. There is another teaching video there, along with at least (usually) two other practice activities, says Taylor.

"However, sometimes we access those activities just because they go along with what we'd like to do that day. Example: There may be a Jeopardy game in the RA folder that the co-teacher would like to play with the class as a review before the mastery assignment, etc."

"Lindsey usually likes to access the activities in the RA folder. . . she likes to let her students do as many activities as possible in each lesson," says Lancaster, and Taylor elaborates on this point, explaining that she often likes to employ repetition as a teaching tool, and digging into the remediation folder offers that possibility, while keeping her students interested in material that they went through before, using different lessons and material.

Moreover, they may be asked to repurpose something they have done on paper into an online or software format. "What we did on paper, for instance, they'll have to put on PowerPoint, and then put in their computer," says Taylor.

"She [the online co-teacher] might send them a link or a game or a video to reinforce that concept. If someone is really struggling they will send them something extra, because the course is individualized; they love these classes," Taylor remarks.

Because the basic outline of class activities—starting with the login, looking at the announcements, looking at feedback from the off-site teacher, and progressing through activities in the different folders—does not change from grade to grade, Taylor finds that "by tenth grade they are great, they know the routine, and they can follow along and participate very well. In ninth grade, I'm talking about rules and procedures. We do things slowly and we log in slowly. I'll say, 'You have a special username, and a special password, and this is where you keep that.' Gradually they learn the entire routine," she says.

Note-taking is guided, which means that students are taking notes either on paper sheets or online that look like worksheets; some words are missing, and they will fill in those blanks as they listen to audio, watch a video, or do research online. So, for example, Taylor may show a video on the smart board, and then circulate as students fill in their guided note sheets. After that, they may log in and take a quiz on the computer, which may provide instant feedback, or might be graded by the co-teacher within the twenty-four-hour grading window.

"I think that the key to this course is also the key to their success: everything addresses the same goal and keeps them engaged, and they don't get bored," Lindsey comments, noting that interaction with the material, whether online or on paper, is important. "Actually 'DOING it' instead of just talking about it or looking at it, helps my students, so online labs or online games are great tools to help my students learn," Taylor responded to me, in her original teacher cohort survey.

FOSTERING LEARNING: MATHEMATICS

Taylor notes that, as special-needs students, she's expected to advocate for them as individual learners, and she's mindful that within the regimented, heavily routinized curriculum they need to express their creativity, and their individuality. A financial management unit, exploring how to budget for living expenses based upon different salaries, offers an example. Here, students could choose a job, and that job came with a salary and various choices: whether to take a bus to work, or drive a car; whether to eat out or make dinner at home.

"They have a choice, and they need to feel like they have a choice," observes Taylor. She will model problems for them, and do problems with them on the smart board, while also letting them move forward individually—once she ascertains they are all at the same level of knowledge, and can do the problems. "They like doing the hard concepts together, but if they have to wait on me, they get frustrated, as well."

"We work on common terms, and on combining terms, and that's so difficult for my students, for students to get it. We've talked about how it's a little like if you have the same last name as someone else. Deanna sent a *Super Mario Brothers* game. You had to drop the same terms into a pipe. I could not believe how quickly the students picked up on it," commented Taylor. "And when I used the terminology of the game, and reminded them of the game, they picked up the skill that quickly, and understood it, and that worked for them. The object was who could get to the farthest level; they wanted to talk about that. And they would ask me, 'Can we go back to our own computers and see if we could go to the next level?,' and so when we would do regular math stuff, I would say, 'Think about the pipes,' and that helped a lot. It's hard for them to do math as a group, unless it is a game," Taylor remarked.

Example: "Unit 1, Lesson 1, in the Introductory Math course teaches the students about integers, absolute value, comparing integers, the number line, etc.," explains Lancaster. "The mastery assignment for that lesson asks the students to print off a sheet of paper with a vertical number line off to the right and create a sea scene. The students are supposed to follow a set of directions such as, "Draw sea level on your paper" (at 0 on the number line), "Draw a whale on your paper. Where did you place him on the number line?" (answer should be a negative number), "Draw a bird on your paper. Where did you place him on the number line?" (answer should be positive), etc. If the students do not enjoy the drawing, or do not feel like they can draw the items requested, we provide pictures they can cut out, instead. This type of activity engages them but also allows us to see if they fully understand positive and negative integers."

"The way that [these] classes are set up, there are notes, quizzes, completion activities, mastery assignments, graphs. We are working on mastery assignments, graphs, and different ways to represent data, such as dot plot, frequency table, and the students are going to have to master these. [Before blended learning] I did it on the dry erase board initially. I want to do it on my computer, so I'm going to let the smart board show it," says Taylor.

FOSTERING LEARNING: SCIENCES

In science, the blended nature of online and hands-on learning is evident. Taylor's small groups do a variety of labs, games, and exercises—some on computer, and some not—to help learn the material.

"We do hands-on labs; and they're working with materials like other regular students would, and like nondisabled students would do. We also do labs online, and the lab is happening on the screen. Sometimes when I taught biology [before], I would let them do it themselves [at their own pace], on a computer, and that was disastrous; everyone was in a different place, and I ran around answering the same question ten times. Now, when they do it together, it helps them understand how the concepts exist, once they see how it works," explains Taylor.

Nevertheless, says Taylor, "it's not all screen work. The students have to create something; they have to create a product. Sometimes they might do a poster, but normally it is on the computer." When students navigate online labs, they sometimes use a Web site called Gizmos, which provides a step-by-step interactive exploration of, for instance, how DNA strands are constructed from amino acids.

Often, Taylor notes, the nature and complexity of the subject matter, and the learning task, will help her decide whether to use digital media, or traditional media, in a particular activity, such as a final mastery activity. For example, in some cases, she seeks to vary instruction through varying the media; in other cases, she may determine that the time allotted for the unit, and the breadth of the material for which the student must demonstrate mastery, determine the use of one kind of media over the other.

But, especially because she wants to share whatever students do with all the stakeholders, whether parents or colleagues, Taylor tries to digitize the students' work. For instance, in applied science, students created posters on posterboard about endangered species—a mastery, or final, assignment in a unit. After researching the animal on the Internet, each student created a poster about an endangered animal—bonobo, Sumatran tiger, North Chinese leopard. Taylor took pictures of the finished projects, and of the students holding them, and created a video presentation, set to music, using Animoto—a popular presentation tool. Applied science was co-taught with NCVPS teacher Karla Tucker, so Taylor shared that video on her site, and e-mailed it to Tucker.

In biology, students created digital presentations about cells, and one student set the parts of the cell to music he selected on the Internet. The specific assignment was "to use the vocabulary from the unit, choose an appropriate picture to represent the vocabulary word chosen, and make the presentation interesting and creative using a template from the site, and music," explains Taylor.

"For science vocabulary, we play a vocabulary game on Quizlet called Scatter. There's a practice, and we do it on the smart board; we learn, we practice it, but every student has to do it. The students then play the game on their own computer," she says. "The person who does it best is 'Scatter champ.' They want to get the lowest time. At the end of every lesson there is a quiz, and they can see their grade as soon as they do it."

Taylor notes, "It makes them take ownership of it, and they have to know the information. It also helps me to figure out what they will eventually understand; the students don't normally skip ahead and look at the activities."

When the science activity involves a hands-on lab, Taylor says she is more likely to use groups of students. It depends on the lab as to whether Taylor will print out a paper copy of the lesson, or "tell them to bring the document up on their computer and fill it in," as they make their way through the steps of the lab.

So, for example, a lab that dealt with volume and displacement involved old plastic camera film canisters; they had to find objects, and make one float, and make one sink. With that lab, Taylor had students fill out a piece of paper, because they were working with a variety of materials, including water—so it was better to avoid using the computer for a few minutes. Another lab did not include any fluids or chemicals—it focused on natural selection and involved students timing each other performing eight different actions, like tying a string, writing their names, and taping their thumbs to their other fingers. "For that one, I didn't print it [the lab lesson] out; they could just fill it in on the computer," says Taylor.

Groups also shift some of the teaching burden to her students. "If I teach my students a concept, and then they can teach their peers the same material, then I consider that a successful learning experience. Especially working with special education students, I have students who learn some concepts easier than others, and some who struggle. I have found that doing the Gizmos together [as a group] is the best way to help them understand the material. Starting out together allows them to, later in the online lab, do some portions on their own," she says.

"I do it on the smart board, and they do exactly what I do on their individual computers, while they watch me, because the labs are virtual. Each person gets their own results, though, because everything doesn't always come up the same way. We can talk more about this, and I can explain. They are required to answer questions as we go along, to fill in questions on their accompanying worksheet, and complete tables that give the data. This gets turned in to the online teacher to be graded," Taylor says.

However, "once they see how to do it, they can do it on their own. They write it down on their worksheets; some of the assignments get sent to the online teacher, and some of the assignments get sent to me."

NETWORKING AND PROFESSIONAL DEVELOPMENT

In some ways, Taylor is engaging in constant professional development via her daily working relationship with Lancaster. She and Lancaster are required to meet in real time, electronically, once per week. When that is added to the regular communication they engage in, professional learning takes place for Taylor each week. She attends conferences and meetings, as well.

Kelli Howe, the assistant principal, says, "Lindsey attends the professional development, and we give her the time off, and support that financially. She also goes to workshops, which can be a couple of days each." For Howe, the costlier and more political investment was "providing the equipment for that to happen, and with North Carolina's [tight education] budget, that is a very big deal."

During early 2013, Taylor took time out of her schedule to develop a history course, American History I, along the lines of the courses she teaches with NCVPS support. NCVPS put together a team of eight professionals—pairs of special education teachers and history teachers—along with two course development supervisors. Taylor was able to provide her perspective on both co-teaching and achieving success with the model, while helping to create a new course with subject-qualified instructors.

Taylor experienced the world of different subject matter from her own world of science and math—in this case, the era from European exploration of North America to post–Civil War Reconstruction. She provided perspective to her teacher-partner about whether vocabulary was pitched correctly to special-needs students, and developed guided notes for them.

Taylor describes an intensive five-month process, starting at the beginning of 2013, and ending in June of that year. It involved one face-to-face meeting and many online meetings. Her team partner worked in a different part of the state. "It was really hard, and really time-consuming . . . This has to align with the Common Core. With occupational kids, they have to have two social studies classes to graduate. They could have taken any history class before and it would have been an inclusion class," she explained.

"He [her partner] did the videos, and the instructional presentations. I did the guided notes, and all the vocabulary, and then we had deadlines: 'The presentations are due in two weeks,' he would e-mail. He's a regular history teacher," without special education training, explained Taylor. "I would say, 'Don't say agricultural, saying farming; this needs to be bold, or underlined,' . . . things that I knew the kids would need," she said.

ASSESSING

Much in the way that Taylor's teaching is continually infused with professional development, so her lessons are a series of continuing assessments. That reflects the blended learning environment and the partnership between NCVPS and Ashbrook, which requires constant electronic communication and evaluation. As Taylor reminds me, "My students take online assessments for each lesson and unit."

Typically, Lancaster and other remote co-teachers will grade overnight any student assignments from Taylor's class—and other classes. "Every night I get online; some assignments are graded automatically in Blackboard, and I usually give [written] feedback [electronically, on student assignments]," explains Lancaster. "They might do a screenshot with a winning screen [from a game]." Students can also use a number of other applications and tools to show mastery of subject matter. They can create a voice-threaded presentation using Voki, or Toondoo, or Wobook—all of which provide online slide shows and presentations, with a few more bells and whistles. The students then attach that file to an e-mail and send it to Lancaster.

"There are lots of options for the kids," she says.

Taylor notes that assessment results have improved dramatically for final and high-stakes examinations since the blended learning partnership with NCVPS was instituted for algebra and biology. "In 2010–2011, the students were in an inclusion setting for both algebra and biology, and none of the students passed the End of Course exams. In 2011–2012, I began teaching NCVPS blended learning classes for the Occupational students, and they still had to take the End of Course exam. One in ten passed biology, and none out of ten passed algebra. They could take these over," recalls Taylor.

"In 2012–2013, I taught the same courses, and eleven of twelve passed the biology exam, fall [10th grade], and eight out of eight passed the Algebra I exam [10th grade]. I also taught applied science [9th graders/fall] through the NCVPS blended learning program, and this was the first year of MSLs [Measurements of Student Learning], state tests, but different from End of Course exams, and ten out of ten passed the exam," she noted.

Taylor comments, "I think there are two reasons for the difference in results. One was that the exam changed. The first year, the students took the regular End of Course exam that all algebra and biology students in the entire state took. The next year, there was a special education version of the exam called the NCExtend2 exam. The content is the same—the students are tested on the same concepts and material, but the test is given online, and there are three answer choices instead of four for each question. Also, there may be fewer questions, like sixty instead of eighty. The other reason for a difference in scores is that I covered a lot more of the material the second year I taught the courses, and this year, since it is my third year, I have covered even more material. I taught the entire biology course this year for the first time."

Meanwhile, Taylor notes that the fairly constant stream of formative assessments, like five-question quizzes, are not high-stakes; students can and do take them over. "The quiz they can take three times;

sometimes they do really poorly at first. Then there's a twenty-question post-assessment. They do pretty well on the post-assessment. Teachers dumb down stuff—I present it to them. They stay engaged."

She also notes that it helps students to be able to do more than just take online quizzes. And, even then, they are graded quickly, which she notes is incredibly important. Her special-needs students always know—as do their parents, via the online grading portal—how they are doing.

"Other assignments, they [students] create something and submit it . . . half are things that they turn into me, on their computers. They can click on a tab, My Grades. The online teachers have to grade within twenty-four hours, with a little feedback [such as] . . . 'Look back over the notes,'" says Taylor.

"We send progress reports home every three weeks," she adds. "I have really good communication with most parents, by e-mail, texting, and calls. It's a hard copy and they have to sign it. In our county, we have the parent assistance model, and parents can go to the portal and log in. It connects to messages, or a phone call: 'Progress reports were sent home today.'"

LESSONS LEARNED

Howe commented, "It's been remarkable to see the strides . . . The NCVPS teacher is phenomenal, but having Lindsey there as the support and following [on] to what they are learning at the NCVPS site is crucial. In some cases, they [students] are all still working at their own pace, and they will come together to work on a lab or on a cell project, and then they will go back to working at their own pace. It's an ideal situation because they are team teaching."

Taylor has the flexibility to adjust her teaching practice as needed, says Howe: "If she feels she needs to follow up [a lesson], she can then do so, but in a different way."

Howe notes that a teacher like Taylor has a "learning curve" when it comes to teaching in a blended setting like the one at Ashbrook. That learning curve, continues Howe, involves understanding how the class content is delivered, how to navigate the Internet for both administrative and teaching tasks, and how to communicate with the online teacher in an efficient way, while making sure that students are able to access and understand all the feedback and graded materials they are getting.

Once the classroom teacher is acclimated to the blending teaching model, says Taylor, they can leverage the technology to great effect. "The variety of activities, and how quickly paced it is, really contributes to their success."

9

Learning as an Experiment

Steven Eno

NINTH TO TWELFTH GRADE
ENGINEERING AND PHYSICS
El Segundo High School, El Segundo, California

When Steven Eno took a job teaching engineering and physics at El Segundo High School (ESHS), near Los Angeles, he went right back to the future. Eno graduated from ESHS in 2002, and was hired in 2010 to help beef up the school's STEM offerings. School officials believed that, even without formal teacher training, at the time, Eno's technology background as a software systems consultant, and his engineering degree from Johns Hopkins, would help boost efforts to interest students in STEM, shepherd them through the program, and help accelerate technology integration at ESHS.

They were rewarded many times over: Eno has upgraded the program with his colleagues, introduced technology to both the learning and teaching sides of his courses, and helped students apply some of what they are learning through participation in Maker Movement competitions, winning or placing in a number of them.

Eno teaches these sciences across the spectrum of grades and levels, while working with his colleagues to implement changes driven by Common Core and technology integration efforts. He is part of a multipronged drive in his district to boost STEM achievement, as well as postgraduate success in related undergraduate programs, using technology, innovative instruction, and inter- and intra-class collaboration. In the summer of 2013, he worked with scientists at a national Jet Propulsion Laboratory to bring some of their work to classrooms.

The administrators who hired Eno saw something else: an energetic educator who would work with the large minority population coming from outside the district to give them a shot at success with STEM studies, and a chance to go to college and boost their post-graduation incomes in jobs requiring technological knowledge and skills. Eno fits the bill—he works with a range of students, from advanced engineering students to those students who are just being introduced to high-school-level STEM.

SINCE JOINING ESHS, Eno has helped revamp the physics and engineering curricula and has worked with math teachers to help overhaul their program as they prepare for Common Core standards implementation. Eno has also set up a tech-based tutoring relationship between his students and UCLA engineering undergraduates, had his classes work with other classes outside California via remote technology, taken his classes to competitions where they demonstrate robots they have built using kits and 3-D printers, and developed with other teachers an application to help students self-manage their science coursework progress. He maintains relationships with nearby corporations that provide facilities and hardware on loan to his programs, while partnering with other teachers to foster collaboration among El Segundo students.

Says Eno, "I think the key to using technology is to make sure the benefit is clear to students; the key is that their learning experience is personalized through technology."

To manifest his "keys" to teaching, Eno joins his colleagues in connecting with area universities for tutoring for his students, to local corporations for hardware, to teachers and technologists working to develop learning software of all kinds, and perhaps most importantly, to his own students, for their feedback on various applications, Web sites, platforms, and curricula. Other summertime projects have seen Eno testing a university-developed program on his own, and then giving his students a shot at it, and working to bring another scientist-created information product to schools. On top of that, he trains annually with the authors of the curriculum he uses in many of his classes.

Collaboration among and between students is taken to new heights, with students having taken part in collaborations between one of his classes and a class in Oregon. Other internal collaborations are being planned.

RAMPING UP

Eno is technologically savvy, and this gives him a leg up in both establishing what he thinks he might need to do his job, and holding those conversations with key school and district technology personnel. He's in close touch with the school's information technology personnel. And he obtains lots of ideas from fellow teachers.

He networked with the area corporations that ESHS had been lobbying for funds, hardware, and access to devices, like 3-D printers, which the school could not afford, but which it wanted to use as it began the process of expanding its STEM offerings. Those printers, and some robotics kits, came in handy when Eno began taking some teams to competitions in which students demonstrate working models they have made. iPads arrived last year, and as of last summer he had developed an iPad application to streamline student management of their coursework. "I have a head start, since I have computers in my class and have already been using technology heavily in physics," says Eno.

"My students do virtual labs every unit on the Web site PhET, and I have them check out lots of other resources. Each unit, my students also complete an engineering project where they are using Vernier probes and software to make measurements. A lot of my students are using 3-D modeling to complete their big projects to determine how they need to create things like roller coasters and to also help them with the physics piece. I am starting to experiment with Wolfram Alpha and many other apps for my students to use to interact with the material," he told me, last year. Wolfram Alpha is a computational search engine that presents calculated answers, and can test the ability of the user to formulate a well-structured question.

Computer-aided design (CAD) and modeling software are now standard software in many school science programs across the country. But it's clear that the Maker competitions he and his students enter are illustrative of a strategy Eno effects in a number of ways: connecting the material to his students' interests, and connecting the students, and their questions, to the wider world. That might involve collaborating with students in another classroom, or school, through various communications technologies, or it might mean obtaining help from college students, using the Web. It may mean looking at physics and engineering examples in popular movies.

He uses what's available, but has learned that some devices and programs work better than others. He has welcomed the iPads into his engineering program, because some of the applications "force investigation" by students, and that increases their interactivity with the subject matter. Instead of consuming the content, they are working with it.

Eno works "closely with the math department to tie the math curriculum closely to the engineering and physics curriculum. We have integrated lots of technology into our practice as a math and physics group," he explained early last year, as he described meeting every other week with a committee of educators preparing for the Common Core standards for math, with a focus on integrating technology. "Everyone that meets in the group was just given a class set of iPads, and we are in the process of setting up all the apps for the class."

"I am constantly looking for new technology to use in the classroom. Whenever I come across something I test it out on my own to see if it would be helpful. Once I find a way to fit technology into a lesson, I just give it to my students. I think this is key—just don't be afraid of getting it perfect and let the students experiment. More times than not my students find new ways to use the technology that I didn't think of," reflects Eno. "For instance this summer [2013] I worked with UCLA and Arizona State [University] to test a new systems analysis software to use in my physics class. Once I heard about the opportunity, I signed up and trained with the software for a few days over the summer. I found a way to use it with my first unit, and I let my students start to play with it. After my students use the technology I always make sure to get a reflection from [them] to see how it could be improved." In this case, Eno says, "I found out my students wanted to create their own problems instead of following given steps. The students are a key part of the process."

He continues, "The software was designed to help students understand system modeling that involved rates of change. The developers envisioned the software would be used for students to work through basic examples involving one-dimensional changing distance, changing velocity, and a constant acceleration. I pushed my students to create their own problems involving rates of change as complex as water bottle rockets where they had a changing mass, changing pressure, and two-dimensional changing acceleration, changing velocity, and a changing distance."

"During reflections I always ask students what helped them the most and what they would change about tools and about lessons. I do this as often as I can so I can get a feel for what works for the class. In this case my sentiment was confirmed that the example problems that the developers put into the software were too easy for the students. They also explained that the software was too confusing to develop their own modeling problems. I thought that they would be able to figure out the development process, but it turned out they struggled just as other teachers during training struggled."

All of this software exploration does not mean paper is entirely eliminated. But its presence and importance has lessened. Eno had thought about junking engineering notebooks last school year. These are still around, while he has focused on increasing administrative efficiencies by using as much of the technology infrastructure as possible to shift graded assignments to the digital space.

Comments Eno, "We have gone mostly paperless in my classes. I am using a combination of Google Docs and the new learning management system [LMS] that PLTW [Project Lead the Way] rolled out this year. Students are submitting assignments and I am grading them through the LMS. We still have engineers' notebooks in engineering and lab books in physics for the students to do calculations and graphs, but other than that most everything is done online."

Later Eno told me, the engineering notebooks "are only used for the initial steps of our engineering design process. Students will do brainstorming, initial sketches, and document project management [timeline, responsibilities, etc.] in their engineering notebook when starting a project. They will also include decision matrices and key decision points for the project in their notebook, and they will refer back to it and document anything that has a drastic change throughout the project. Once they have this initial documentation, they move to CAD modeling and online documentation to create more organized and final documentation. Students now take notes online and manage all other class materials online."

Eno has a class set of iPads, and access to a full suite of desktops; the school is fully Internet-connected. Eno has also "converted an additional fifteen laptops to run Ubuntu so that students can get a feel for a different OS and try some additional programming. I haven't had the chance to integrate programming into my physics class yet, but I am continuing to try."

However, Eno did experiment with the national "Hour of Code," a movement that encouraged teachers to let students try their hands at writing computer code. "It was huge in all my classes and introduced everyone to programming. I even got twenty other teachers to try it out, and all of their students loved it; most of them have never heard of engineering or computer science."

MATCHING LEARNING GOALS AND TECHNOLOGY

Eno searches the Internet constantly for ideas about how to engage his students in the complex content that he teaches in both physics and engineering, and once engaged, he makes an effort to use applications, software, and games that challenge students to think more deeply about the discipline's core operations rather than technology that delivers content in the form of explanations or problems, with no real-world application or interactivity.

He says that means he stays away from software that just puts up equations on the screen, or very basic videos that detail the information but offer no interactive possibilities. From his perspective, technology that assists and directly helps students to work with the concepts in a way that promotes understanding, and ultimately independent application of them—whether it be wave energy or kinematics—is the best kind of technology to integrate into his classrooms. He's also looking for the technology to provide the foundation for verbalizing and writing about the sciences that he is teaching.

He favors interactive software that they can play with, and engage with the material, before "I even launch into an explanation." And, it's for that reason that Eno has experimented with a technology-centric version of the standard "investigation before explanation" (IBE) science teaching method. But no app is a magic wand.

The IBE method, explains Eno, "gives students a chance to interact with the material and try to solve a problem before they are given notes and [an explanation of] exactly what the concepts are. This gives them a purpose to pay attention when given new material, and shows them they still have room to grow."

Currently, "We have experimented with running IBEs on iPads. This is most helpful when we have students playing a game, or running a virtual lab individually. There are some great apps like 'Educreations,' where students can write and record their voice at the same time, which helps get an understanding of how they approach problems. For the most part the IBEs still run the best with whiteboards and dry erase boards because of the flexibility," he offers.

Still, Eno noted, during the first school year, with all of the technology available, some basic tools of his class remained on paper, like the engineering notebooks. He's hoping to get rid of the paper version, to make notes easier to share, to be able to check in easier from his screen, on note-taking. Now, he just walks around and looks at the notebooks quickly. Handouts and notes are sometimes lost, or left at home, rather than always being online, or in the student's electronic portfolio. However, some students have leapt ahead to an electronic world on their own. Even as he was contemplating shifting the notebooks to the electronic versions, "some students did everything on Google Drive, on their own, and then shared it with me, so I could see their notes," he recalled.

"My big thing is to find ways to extend the students' learning beyond what I can normally provide by myself. I try to stay away from those apps that just ask them to figure out an equation, or a video. I want them to use something in which they can see how waves are affected by energy—an additional experience that extends their understanding of that experience. And to find creative ways for students to connect to physics, because physics can be explained in so many different ways."

Regarding IBE, adds Eno: "In terms of order, I want them to be hooked into the material" first, before he begins problem solving and working through the guts of the concepts, by either "watching a video or playing a game." This is "tying them into the material they really enjoy, and then going into some kind of interaction" with the content "before I even start explaining," he says.

Basically, explains Eno, "I want them to engage" with the material, "and also it gives me a picture of how they are" and what their attitude and level of interest is toward material.

"So, hooking them first, and then letting them investigate" is the way he approaches many lessons. "It helps define what I need, in terms of lecture notes, and what I do after my lecture; I have a really loose lesson plan. The data that my students give me helps me develop it; not on the fly, but with a little more detail. Having taught for [more than] three years, I know what to look for."

Problem solving has a place, but so does creating presentations and working on real-life problems. Much has been advanced by giving kids access to sophisticated kinds of CAD software—as at ESHS. One important piece of curriculum is provided by Project Lead the Way, a nationally recognized nonprofit developing STEM curriculum. El Segundo uses PLTW, and Eno attends their summer training sessions. PLTW provides a lot of curricular support, including materials and training. Nevertheless, Eno takes that curriculum and tweaks it, based upon what he knows about his students, to include lessons that will help in entering all of the Maker competitions.

"All of our engineering classes are PLTW classes. PLTW gives teachers the curriculum and the training to teach the classes. We don't have to do exactly what the curriculum says, but it gives us a great baseline to start with. I have modified the curriculum quite a bit to enter more Maker type of competitions such as Vex, and now, a Popsicle stick bridge-building contest run by the American Society of Civil Engineers," he explains.

There is a lot of experimentation in Eno's teaching life. Working to increase the number of virtual games with an educational purpose, "I tried to set up a classwide role-playing game [RPG] at the beginning of the year where students would choose a role—Defender, Attacker, Alchemist, etc.—and work on leveling up their skills through practice problems, labs, etc. I had an intricate system based on the many *Final Fantasy* RPG systems, but couldn't get it off the ground."

DIFFERENTIATING AND FOSTERING INDEPENDENT LEARNING

How do you choose what to incorporate in a lesson? How Eno chooses the technology is driven by a combination of factors, including the standards he must cover, and what's available, which will address his pedagogical philosophy of "extending their experience beyond what he can do for them," as one ESHS administrator told me. As importantly, Eno works at "de-geek-ifying" his subject matter by trying to connect it to student interests outside the classroom—something ESHS administrators had asked him to focus on from the beginning.

So, for Eno, his interest is in making sure students are personally invested in wave theory, or kinematics, which means that he needs to randomly survey students about personal interests. This personal information plays a big role in how he directs his lessons, and which branch of the lesson he is likely to travel down. Eno has asked them about their favorite movies from different decades, and their favorite gaming apps on mobile devices, among other things.

In previous years he has employed a decidedly low-tech approach that, in the context of his classes, actually provides a change. It's quick, it's easy, and it's simple.

"One word on stickies," he explains. "I survey my students about a specific interest I have chosen simply by giving each student a sticky note and having them write down their favorite. This specific interest I will use as a starting point for the rest of my lesson, and it could range from sports, video games, movies, music, phone apps, etc. I usually stick to pop culture because that is the focus of most teenage lives."

What comes back can send him, and his students, down a number of branches, many of which do involve some kind of technology, such as 3-D modeling software, now widely available to students from computer-aided draft software makers, like Autodesk. It also means that when they use the technology, he may be able to give them a choice about what they pursue. Should they create a roller coaster? Or, a bike rack?

In Eno's Engineering Design and Development (EDD) class, "my senior engineering class has to gather data for potential problems they are solving. They use online surveys because they need much more data than just one word," he notes. "This survey is actually a critical starting point for the whole year, and the students revisit it multiple times. EDD isn't structured like most classes in that there aren't lessons or units to organize the class. This is really a senior design class that allows the students to work for a year on solving a problem they choose. The survey piece helps them, one, determine if a problem exists; two, refine their thoughts on solutions; three, see if their solution works for consumers. The students have typically used SurveyMonkey, or a similar online tool, to conduct their survey and analyze the data. They get their survey out to the public mostly through Facebook, Twitter, and other social networks."

To connect students with subject matter, he must also connect with his students. As he tells it, this can involve some performance art, as well as videos and technology.

"One example of the pedagogical order that I use is for my lesson of kinematics. I first hooked the students by surveying them for their favorite phone app. Their response was *Bloon's Tower Defense*. I then had them play *Bloon's Tower Defense* on the iPads and gave them specific things I wanted them to observe—how long they had to pop the bloons, differences between bloons, etc. I gave them a few sentence starters that I wanted them to complete so I knew they would write down something. After that I gave them a chance to hit me with a water balloon launcher. I didn't tell them how they would do it, but that they would only get three tries. This investigation gave them the chance to think through 2-D kinematics and how the acceleration due to gravity affects the path of the water balloon. I again gave them specific observations I wanted them to make so that they were thinking through the physics behind what was going on with the water balloon."

"I did not get hit by water balloons in this class. Since it was treated more as an IBE, they didn't have all the information they needed to hit me. I did get them hooked to learn about 2-D kinematics and projectile motion. All I did to set this up was sit in a chair thirty yards from a water balloon launcher [three-person launcher made out of surgical tubing] and a bucket of water balloons, and I gave them fifteen minutes to try and hit me."

"I do this with my physics class as a unit-ending lab, and I was hit three times this year. In physics, the hook involved defending the Earth from invaders. I surveyed the students about their favorite superhero movie this year [the 2013–2014 school year], and *Avengers* was their favorite. I showed them the clip of the invading aliens and asked them to diagram how they would protect the world. This gave them a first look at projectile motion," recounts Eno.

FOSTERING COLLABORATION AND COMMUNICATION

Eno notes that his students are "rarely working on anything individually." One key to connecting subject matter to students, in his view, is to also connect students to other students. The rigor of communicating questions, problems, solutions, and challenges between people who are not known to you, helps develop communication skills in disciplines that have not always been known for encouraging those skills. Working together remotely boosts the level of challenge, but also the level of critical thinking required to participate in these activities, Eno says.

In a previous year, Eno worked with Philip Hayes, a teacher at Skyview High School, in Vancouver, Washington. The task for both their classes of engineering students was to design a bicycle rack online and in partnership with student groups; students used webcam, Skype, and e-mail to work together and communicate. Eno's choice of assignment and technology, in collaboration with his opposite number in Washington, centered around a commonplace piece of hardware in students' lives, many of whom own bicycles and few of whom have driven cars— or if they have, not for long. Knowing teens can learn from each other, and like socializing, it was easy to get students to cam and Skype with their remote partners.

How it happened: "Phil and I met virtually before the project started and hashed out what tools the students would use. Webcam and Skype were key, along with e-mail, Google Docs, and Dropbox. Now we are using Autodesk 360 [cloud-based 3-D modeling file storage]. We both used our past experiences with technology to help decide what technology we would use. Phil and I met weekly to make sure the project ran smoothly. We used spreadsheets to track student interactions and progress. We also had students 'cc' us on all e-mail correspondence so that we could get ahead of any tension, and so the students would keep communication professional. Students ended up meeting outside of class on Facebook and Xbox Live, which was pretty cool."

Students can also learn from students working at the university level. Students in Eno's AP physics class have sought out tutoring from an innovative, asynchronous program, offered by UCLA. Through this program, engineering undergraduates tutor Eno's students by answering questions they have posted on a message board run by the UCLA program.

William Herrera runs the UCLA side of the program as the education coordinator for UCLA's Office of Academic and Student Affairs, Henry Samueli School of Engineering and Applied Science. Herrera noted last summer [2013] that there are a number of challenges making the program useful, including getting teachers to upload course information, and getting students to frame questions in a way that tutors can quickly apprehend what they need. In Eno's case, Herrera said, Eno has created an online forum just for this project, which helps everyone in providing the tutoring service.

"We go over with the teachers how to set up his course [online], how to upload his course, and then the hardest part is to frame their [students'] questions the right way. Sometimes they type it out word for word. I encourage them to take photos [of the problems] with their phones, so they can properly word their questions, and to keep in mind that the tutor doesn't always have the same resources as the student, such as the textbook, or the problem set. The more resources they upload, the better. I also encourage tutors to communicate directly with Steven, almost like a course TA [teaching assistant]," says Herrera.

ASSESSING

No matter how much technology is used, a question can remain about how much critical thinking has taken place, and how much is retained. In Eno's class, the goal is not to impress with just displays, such as PowerPoint slides, but with the thoughts those displays engender.

This leads to the question he poses to all his students: how do you use slides not as a crib sheet, but as a backup? It's actually an important skill for speaking in the wider world, whether talking about aerodynamics, Charles Dickens, or profit and loss. Using multimedia does not allow Eno's students to escape explaining their work, or their thought process about the work they just did with each other. They may create a whiz-bang slide set, and they can e-mail or share that set with Eno when they are done presenting, but they have to engage in critical thinking about the concepts depicted in the set.

"They know they are not supposed to just rely on the slides; they also know I will ask probing questions," reminding one that verbalizing and writing about scientific understanding—and being able to refer back to all of that online, if possible—is just as important as the solving of problem sets and equations.

But the question remains—how to move kids forward?

At one point, earlier in the interviews with Eno, he said, "I don't give them enough feedback along the way; that's a place where I struggle." A partial solution to this, and one that also has broader implications for helping students keep up with the work, is a long-term project Eno has pursued. In concert with other teachers at ESHS, he spent part of last summer [2013] developing an iPad application that will help students track their own progress, and the coursework milestones that they must meet as they make their way through his classes. But, it will be more than a scheduler. Eno hopes it will help them set up learning targets, and they can then access notes for particular units, with "branches" if students need extra help in understanding and applying concepts.

"The idea is that students are owning more of the project work, and owning more of their own progress," opines Eno. "We're hoping that by all them having class goals, notes and handouts won't get shoved in a notebook somewhere. It will answer questions for them like 'Do you need help? If so, try this app, try viewing this video.'"

Always be prepared: by last fall (2013), with the app still being tested, Eno and colleagues rolled out a paper version to introduce, at least, the concept of the app, as a bridge to its final rollout. Later, during the 2013–2014 school year, he made enough progress on the app to give it a name—Grasp—and to begin testing a beta version of it, at school.

As of the middle of the 2013–2014 school year, Eno explains, "Our Web app, called Grasp, is going great. We are in the second iteration of Grasp and getting some amazing data. Initially we had a very rough version that was mainly used for my class and one other teacher's class. We have made many changes in the details of our grading and tracking this year, so our initial version was constantly in flux. This beta version is now in testing with four classes and running much smoother. Students can input their goal level for a concept and then input their mastery level after an assessment. This gives them a clear view of where they need to work and helps teachers identify what students need help and with what concepts. I am still working with programmers to implement graphing and some visualization of progress, but it is coming along well. We are hoping to have a final version for the whole school and other schools ready to go next year with a native iOS app as well."

Rolling "game-ification" into the app is a goal. "Eventually we want to have a medaling system and have students complete missions by leveling up. I have played with some versions of this outside of the app, but nothing is complete yet," he explains.

Notable is that Eno found that even with the prelaunch paper version of the app, students appreciated the additional progress-charting, noting that it was "helping students understand their own learning progress and create next steps to help them master concepts," with the result being that he and other teachers saw "much more targeted work in class."

NETWORKING

Although Eno does not teach math, he has taken part in a working group of math teachers reorganizing the curriculum to more closely align their efforts with the Common Core. That group have all received iPads, and Eno participated in the effort to pick applications for it, and set those up. This gave him cross-curricular perspective on his own practice as it relates to physics, knowing what—and how—students are being taught in a related discipline, mathematics.

During the summer, Eno also worked at the NASA-funded Jet Propulsion Laboratory, in Pasadena, California, helping to make available an information product for classroom use. "The product is called Eyes on the Solar System [http://eyes.nasa.gov/] and is an amazing product that uses real-time engineering data from their satellite to show what is going on around the solar system. I went through the Next Generation Science Standards and showed how the Eyes technology can be used in the classroom."

In addition, explains Eno, Project Lead the Way requires annual training. "I have done PLTW training each summer for all the engineering classes that I teach. The training lasts two weeks and consists of a forty-hour work week, where we go through all the curriculum and use the key pieces of technology—everything from Vex and RobotC to online tools for aerospace analytics—for the class. We also are required to go through each major project on our own so we know what the students go through. These projects are everything from the design projects in IED [Introduction to Engineering Design] to launching model rockets for AE [Aerospace Engineering]."

Networking with other teachers around the country is something that comes naturally to Eno, who is a part of several online-based networking groups. Speaking of game-ification efforts, Eno said, "I have also been in touch with Mike Skocko from Valhalla High School who has created an amazing game-ification system called Game-On. He and his students created it and have been using it, and it's something I would like to implement. I was able to use the Kerbal Space Program in physics, but not as much as I wanted to, because it didn't work well on my set of laptops. I am experimenting with the MIT Radix system, but I have not used it in class. I am a part of a game-ification community through edWeb, but unfortunately have not had time to be as active as I would like."

Professional development opportunities sometimes arise spontaneously, and Eno works around scheduling issues. "For my EDD class, I didn't go through the summer training with Project Lead the Way, like I have with my other classes . . . Instead of going to training I spoke to multiple teachers who taught the class to see what works and what doesn't work. I also stumbled upon a free online class through Stanford titled Technology Entrepreneurship."

He will apply the lessons from Technology Entrepreneurship in future ESHS classes. "It was an amazing class that taught programming and business, and I have adopted it as a key part of my EDD class. I am making each [class] group act as a startup, to come up with their own product and raise funding for their idea," explains Eno.

10

Summing Up

New Paradigms for Teaching and Learning

TEACHING IS COMPLEX AND ITERATIVE. Technology is quite fluid. Because of this and the general pace of change within many schools, I often felt, in speaking with these teachers and others about their practice—despite the standard high-tech tools of communication at my disposal, including online note-taking software—like the colonial-era correspondent, who having mailed a letter congratulating someone, finds out much later that the object of the congratulations passed away some months previous.

This phenomenon can be especially true for, but not confined to, science teachers (Craft, Eno, Taylor). And, while many teachers are just dipping their teaching toes in the waters of technology integration—digitizing a worksheet here, or posting a video online there—these teachers are likely to be moving even farther afield into new kinds of collaborative and interactive technologies.

Good teaching, however, based upon solid pedagogy, does not change quite so quickly, and the facets of good teaching that are widely recognized—such as fostering student engagement, scaffolding content through a variety of means, modeling appropriate behavior, especially in cyberspace, tapping into students' organic motivation, and connecting the material to their lives—are consistently on display here, along with many other aspects of exceptional instructional practice. So, the challenge is to elucidate how these good teachers are combining excellent practice with technology.

In looking more closely at the foregoing snapshot of teachers integrating technology in various ways, a number of larger and small truths, a collection of trends, and some notable patterns about their practices, surface and resolve.

NEW RELATIONSHIPS WITH CONTENT AND EACH OTHER

In general, what the teachers have shared about their experiences makes it clear that relationships always integral to K–12 learning in a classroom setting—for instance, the working relationship between teacher and student, and that of the student to the subject matter—have metamorphosed into multiple connections as these teachers used increasing amounts of technology. Call it "multilateralism."

Prior to the advent of the latest wave of Internet-ready technology, either custom-built for the classroom, or repurposed for that environment, the primary learning relationship in the classroom existed between teacher and student. For many classrooms, that is still the case. In this paradigm, learning passed from teacher to student, and then back to the teacher, as a check on the original step, in a heavily prescribed format. The student worked off of whatever was received from the teacher, or the teacher's materials, and reshaping, reiterating, and regurgitating that material in a way that showed familiarity with, and understanding of, the original content as transmitted from teacher to student. Application of that material to other, and perhaps wholly different, contexts, was less important. The teacher-student relationship was in most cases not only the primary professional relationship in the classroom, but the only one. To the extent that students worked with each other, this was to reinforce this primary relationship, and to effect the transmittal of information from teacher to student, and from student back to the teacher, as measured by regular assessments—primarily examinations, and "papers" of one sort or another.

Among the changes that the teachers in this book, and the teaching they discuss, show us, is the changing nature of the relationship of the student to, not just the teacher, but learning in general, as mediated by an increased use of technology. The teachers in this book are increasing their use of technology and impacting this relationship in a number of ways, as by providing more multifaceted channels for learning, by fleshing out the various steps in a lesson to connect in more personal ways with each student, and by expanding the possibilities for achieving and showing mastery. Those steps often do not conform to the standard "sit and get" or "drill and kill" paradigms that have governed much of education for so long.

In a sense, teachers are asking, permitting, and often encouraging students to relate in much greater and broader and deeper ways, with the material, with other students, and even with other classes and information sources—whether people or institutions. Pernille Ripp, Jennifer Motter, Christopher Craft, Lindsey Taylor, and others all ask their students to consider new and different sources for their students' research. Therefore, one trend that is clear among these teachers is the promotion of multilateralism within their classrooms: stronger learning relationships between and among students, and between students and the content itself. They hope that the more seriously students take work with other students, the stronger they will relate to, and master, the content—both together and individually.

Related trends include a propensity for situations that allow and encourage students to interact with the subject matter rather than consuming it passively, including in the introductory phase of a lesson; sharing work with classmates, teachers, and other classes with greater frequency; reflecting upon what is shared, and utilizing that as a launching pad for further instruction and learning; requiring and assessing conversations among and between students, and encouraging conversations between classes; using the technology to encourage question-formation; using it to promote administrative efficiencies in formative assessments and understanding-checks; creating artifacts of student learning that are permanently accessible; developing inquiry and research skills; and game-ifying various learning tasks.

Moreover, the work of learning in K–12 is now, in these classrooms, inextricably linked with learning about how to manipulate the technology used in these classrooms. Students are being asked to practice skills in online researching, and in using a variety of media, tied to this technology, to create something new with the learning they are doing. For these teachers, tweaking technology, using it, and trying something—an application, a Web site, a remote clicker, or creating online forms and testing the turn-in rates among students, or a file conversion—is a part of their routine. It's important to note that integration efforts in all of these classrooms have occurred gradually, and that most of the teachers engage in integration that is additive, rather than immediately transformative. Trying one tech-related activity, and then with positive results, expanding it more widely, in scope or in application, to more classes, seems like a common pattern.

Promotion of student-centered learning, and students taking control of their own learning to a greater extent, have been discussed in earnest for the last few years. There's been a chicken-and-egg quality to these discussions, with some noting that this is an ideal to be pursued when class sizes, schedules, teaching loads, pay, technological resources, and a range of other "stars" align, while others argue that this is, a priori, an ideal supported by voluminous amounts of research, and something to be pursued as part of quality education reform.

Whatever the case, it's clear that teachers integrating technology in a thoughtful manner are moving in the direction of shifting the learning to students themselves. Sometimes radically so, as when Josh Silver's students develop a rubric for their own projects and post that online so it can be downloaded whenever they like, or when Steven Eno's students begin to play with an app that will help them chart their progress, and make decisions about where they need to focus their efforts.

A LAB, NOT A CLASSROOM

What about the technology itself? Several trends present themselves, including the acquisition of technology through private grant-writing efforts, where districts cannot or will not fund technology purchases (Laura Bradley, Josh Stumpenhorst); the growth of bring-your-own-device policies that permit students to utilize their own personal devices, such as smartphones, tablets, and laptops (Christopher Craft, Josh Silver, and others); and the transformation of the classroom into a laboratory-like setting that encourages lab-like behaviors and practices, such as experimentation, inquiry, and analysis.

Once upon a time, technology in schools was mostly found in media centers and computer labs, libraries, and science labs. Now the lab has moved into the classroom, and the laboratory-like setting, and the experience that goes with that is also becoming prominent, as Christopher Craft, Lindsey Taylor, Steven Eno, and others demonstrate. This shift does more, it's clear, than just upgrade the student access to devices, however. It's both promoting and supporting a philosophy of observation, exploration, discovery, and inquiry, that, not coincidentally, is a centerpiece of larger educational reform efforts. Indeed, the practices often undertaken in a lab—experimentation, investigation, observation, analysis, reflection—can be found repeatedly in the lessons of many of the teachers in this book. Notably, laboratory-style work does not take place just in the science classrooms.

In that environment, students learn from each other, and the work of learning shifts onto them as well. Relative to how students work together, it is not clear whether, in the aggregate, more group work, and less whole-class work, takes place within this cohort, but group and partner work feature prominently in their pedagogy. This phenomenon is boosted by the ability for groups to record what they do online, and for teachers to examine what they are doing—through video, through posts, through shared online documents—in a fairly easy way, to progress-check and provide input. As well, with electronic connections like blogs and shared online documents and notes, students can work virtually as partners or small groups, without physically getting together at a table, say, in a classroom or at the library.

Whole-class discussions, work, and lecture have been a tried and true paradigm of K–12 education, even as group work and learning centers began to gain a foothold as alternatives. Group work, partner work, collaboration, independent work, and laboratory-style work were the exception and, even if common, were a break from the default setting: whole-class. While whole-class work does take place among the cohort and their classes, it seems to do so with less regularity than with teachers for whom technology is not as accessible or available. They show less fidelity to the paradigm of whole-class, even as groups of students may be working on the same assignment.

Teachers have been breaking students into collaborative groups for decades. What's new, perhaps, is that they are expected to produce, and share, any results of that group work, which may then be the foundation for any number of other activities and communications, especially response and critique from fellow students. They may be asked to post that presentation, and reflect upon the comments they get from other students, as Josh Silver and many of the other teachers are doing.

It's one thing for schoolchildren to share their work, and then return to their respective "corners" where they proceed to do exactly as their neighbor did—but no one being the wiser, except maybe the teacher, who may or may not discern the similarity. It's another to have students post their work so that the entire class can see it. Typically, when that was artwork, posting it on a wall made sense. But the ability to post other forms of media in a public way has helped to extend that paradigm, and has opened up other avenues for teachers and students to explore.

A COMFORT WITH QUESTIONS

Comfort with open-ended answers, and questions, also features strongly in their pedagogy. As Pernille Ripp, Jennifer Motter, Josh Silver, and most of the other teachers have discovered, the actual educational standards, when held up to the light in isolation from each other, are fairly narrow. With technology, many of the teachers are finding they can flesh them out, push the standard to its creative extreme, link more standards together, encourage more critical thinking in their students, and do double duty on the life-skills front, by teaching digital literacy and developing technology skills within the interplay of teaching and learning. The result, in these classrooms, often seems like chefs combining ingredients in new ways. Accepting a range of responses is not just permitted, but encouraged.

A range of responses can be more appropriate to promoting conversation than it is to promoting traditional whole-class discussion. The older sort of discussion—structured, and proscribed by assignment, and usually led by the teacher—has been a K–12 staple. What we hear from these teachers is the championing of, curiosity about, and support for conversations, especially digital ones, where the artifacts of the interchange remain available for use and study indefinitely, and where the intellectual conclusions drawn by students from those exchanges may, nor may not, be definitive.

Many of the teachers are working to develop digital conversations with their students, and between and among students, with varying degrees of success, and within the context of a range of assignments. The word "conversation" itself implies a give-and-take, and an open-ended quality, that a discussion has often not had, at least within the context of the classroom. It also speaks to the intention of involving as many students as possible in interchanges that previously were, in many cases, the province of a minority of students interested in a whole-class, or even group, discussion.

A DIMINISHED ROLE FOR PAPER

What is the role of paper? The use of paper in these classrooms runs the gamut from occupying a still prominent one (Laura Bradley), to being consciously reduced in use (Christopher Craft), to being used as a way of differentiating and varying instruction (Amber Kowatch and others).

Teachers who are some of the heaviest users of technology (Bradley, Silver, Eno, Kowatch) experiment with various kinds and find that, in some cases, paper, or whiteboards, still work best. This reflects many things: the reality of running a blended classroom, of technology that is a mixture of the twentieth- and twenty-first-century being used within a venue, of paradigms that date in America from the nineteenth century, and of the limits of technology itself, as it now exists.

But it's clear that, rather than being the preeminent media tool, paper is diminished in currency, if not importance, for several reasons. It is less fungible than its digital counterpart, when used in writing by students, and when used as a palette that requires feedback—like Josh Stumpen-horst's "small snapshot grading"—that in structure is more like an iterative conversation than response or reaction. It's less able to support the multimedia annotation of texts and material that is popular, especially when those annotations are meant to be shared with others. And, it is cumbersome to use as an administrative tool—witness the near ubiquity of grading portals accessible to students and parents—along with instant feedback that some teachers have begun obtaining when generating quizzes (Laura Bradley, Steven Eno), or self-assessments, quick surveys ("a word that describes your interests"), and progress charts. Instead, its multidimensional, tactile qualities have come to the fore, for students who prefer it, or for a teacher who sees it as a change from screen work, or as a quick convenience—a free-write paragraph or a quick understanding check—or as a backup. As much material as there is on the Internet for these classes, much material remains in paper format; that situation will shift as more textbooks and sources are digitized.

Moving away from paper offers a way to access a world that only exists beyond its realm: the world of cyber-reviews and aggregative, issue-specific Web sites. This is the world that Josh Silver is helping his students access, but also from which they are learning about both the wider world and how the thinking skills they are practicing can apply to it—whether that is by reading a classic play or by reinventing an instruction manual.

The permanence of learning artifacts—from a teacher's comments on an essay in Google Docs, to the video of a smart-board presentation—remains a fundamental difference from the world of presentations on note cards, and essays handed in and returned with comments in the margins. These artifacts persist, and can be revisited with ease, and provide potentially more meaningful analysis—whether it is the autumn poster, or some word-usage sentences, in a second-grade classroom like that of Amber Kowatch, or the digital presentation in a high school classroom like that of Josh Silver. That is not to say that the digital equivalent of shoving a paper to the back of the hallway locker—poorly named files saved to an equally poorly labeled and located folder—cannot trip up students (or adults, for that matter).

Yet it remains unclear whether paper is truly on its way out in these classrooms. Some teachers, like Christopher Craft and Amber Kowatch, are testing the boundaries of the paper and digital border in their pedagogy all the time—yet they acknowledge that paper has its uses, and that a tactile production by a student has its place. Any paper-based images can be digitally captured, as Lindsey Taylor does for her students' poster presentations.

All this said, and perhaps ironically, paper now offers something in the classroom that computers once did: a way to vary instruction. In this case, the older medium can serve as either a break from the screen, or as a method of reintroducing tactility to the student's learning experience, in the hopes of affecting student cognition, where keyboards and touch-screens may not.

BEYOND "INTO, THROUGH, AND BEYOND"

This brings up the issue of differentiation. It would appear that technology offers more possibilities for differentiation, as managed by a teacher, than previously existed. Although I divided the integration tasks into subjective categories—such as finding ways to use technology to foster collaboration, to match the technology with the learning goals, and to find ways to assess using technology—one overarching task seems to describe a lot of what these teachers do: finding ways to use the available technology so that students can interact with both the material itself (and preferably in some way that is individual to them), and with their fellow students about the material, in a proactive manner that is also individual to the student in some way.

This idea is in some ways not new. The idea of introducing material before starting to do problem solving, whether in physics or English class, has been used for years by teachers who follow the three steps of lesson and unit development known as "into (familiarizing students with the big picture, connecting them and their interests to the materials, hooking them), "through" (the heart of the lesson), and "beyond" (setting up future learning, predicting how current lessons can apply to existing and new course material).

How, at the start of a unit or lesson, to both ease students into new material and connect it with them in a way that ensures they will push past initial discomforts and challenges? It's an age-old problem. What is new are the myriad ways in which that introductory phase can be taught by the teacher, and experienced by the students, as highly interactive. Lessons created by Christopher Craft, Laura Bradley, Steven Eno, and the others indicate that this is an area that continues to grow. Working to familiarize students with the content, and getting their buy-in for the unit lessons—and treating this phase of lesson execution as seriously as the heart of the lesson or the assessment—sets many of these teachers apart. They are leveraging the tech tools at their disposal to do this in many different ways.

There are obviously many ways to break out technology integration tasks for discussion. For example, besides those mentioned above, one might look at how technology is hewing to the basic teaching tasks of contextual planning, lesson creation, instruction, assessment, and reflection. But there is no perfect way to examine technology integration practices, so I chose themes that could be reflected in many, if not most, of the teacher cohort interviewed herein.

Even if one does not accept that technology is offering more ways for students to learn, and teachers to teach, the reality that it could offer some organizational efficiencies for the teacher alone seems supported by these teachers' practices, from online quizzes, to online grading of writing, to conferencing with curriculum developers (Motter, Taylor). It seems like only the beginning for this area of integration, as Craft ably points out, and demonstrates in using technology in both his teaching and the administration of his practice.

Self-adaptive software is an area of growth that Amber Kowatch has experimented with; it's widely used to help students learn foundational concepts in mathematics. Whether that will become true for, say, grammar in language arts classes, remains to be seen. It's already true for reading remediation (for example, the Read180 package). This area of software sets many on edge, wondering whether it diminishes the role of the teacher and augurs some end to the profession. Instead, it's possible to envision a future in which the use of such software for developing basic skill sets will free up teachers to redouble and refocus efforts on higher-order thinking skills as a true facilitator, coach, and guide to the more complex aspects of the subject matter, and to explore with students in a hands-on way more of the project-based learning that features in so much reform curriculum.

NEW PATHWAYS

After all the public battles over the standards, and the teaching of the core subjects of English and mathematics, it can be easy to forget that non-core and special-needs classes are not only using technology, but are using it to push into new areas in creative ways. In the visual arts, access to major museum collections has been available on the Internet for nearly a decade—or more, in some cases. For Jennifer Motter, online galleries are a small piece of a much larger curriculum she is developing to bring the most contemporary digital graphics skills to rural middle school students. Critically, she is utilizing not just her own expertise, but that of her state's university system and art education professionals to enrich her students' learning. That's made possible through an infrastructure she has pieced together with support, over more than a year, from various supportive stakeholders.

Lindsey Taylor's special education classes show that technology is not just something for mainstream students, or for entertaining non-mainstream students. Rather, the approach is to provide a learning hub in cyberspace from which any number of paths can be pursued by both the physical and virtual teachers as they differentiate and fine-tune the curriculum for their exceptional population. It is interesting to note that the learning equation in her classroom includes not only the use of large amounts of technology—something that is acknowledged by all stakeholders as a critical element of her success and that of her students—but also a doubling of human effort in the form of two trained, caring adults who together manage the students' learning and assessment. Her classroom does not necessarily argue for separate education for special-needs children, as much as for supported, and supportive, tech-infused educational arrangements that position these particular students to succeed and achieve. What are they capable of? We, and they, have a better chance at finding out, both in high school and afterwards, because of the intensive and efficient nature of the learning ecosystem in Taylor's classroom, which extends to her remote counterpart.

What can we make of these trends without doing further analysis, of a quantitative nature?

It seems that Common Core values are manifesting in these classrooms, to some extent in tandem with the upgrading of technological infrastructure, and possibly because of the flexibility and power of the technology available to some of the teachers who choose to use it. These teachers talk a lot about the "Four Cs" of the Common Core, whether or not they are thinking about executing the Common Core at any given time (although some are directly involved in curriculum reviews related to Common Core implementation).

"Communication" is one of those Cs. Class can become a continual public performance with all this sharing, and talk about audience; does technology in the classroom reward the extrovert? To a certain extent, many social situations reward the extrovert, regardless of whether that extrovert is a hand-raiser, or an inveterate user of all-caps and exclamation points. But students who could never seem to raise their hand before, who didn't want to, or weren't noticed, can write or create expertly to obtain the attention they deserve, submit a heartfelt video or podcast, or a picture or graphic image that captures what they are trying to say, and how they are trying to connect with and master the material for their use. Student response systems, in the form of clickers, also put achievement on display, without focusing attention on the achiever, honoring their possible need for anonymity. Individual student voices are being heard via voice annotation of slide shows, video, podcasts, and voice clips in many ways, unmediated by the constraints of whole-class discussion or presentation.

While social media dominates the headlines when it comes to communication activities in school, communication appears in these classrooms in many forms, in addition to that of social media: in a presentation by students; in conversations via peer editing and collaborative projects; in reflections by students about their own and others' artworks, and the lessons themselves; in Skype conversations between whole classes of students. Many of the teachers talk about promoting and championing conversations—not just discussion—among and between their students; conversation is a mature, more personal method of learning about the world, and they are showing that, using tech, they can foster these in productive ways.

There is a tendency in current education debates to conflate the pedagogical and the political, nowhere more so than when it comes to standards. What these teachers focus upon are strategies and tactics that will help their students achieve—tech being a tool to do that. So, for them, "collaboration" and "communication" are not just hallmarks of Common Core, but also pathways to greater engagement. Technology assists them in bringing more of this to their classroom, and potentially to convert that engagement to achievement.

COACHING, WITHOUT CARRYING THE BALL

Finally, does technology—once established and used widely—relegate teachers to the sidelines of instruction and education? It would seem instead, at least in these classrooms, to reserve to teachers more of what an adult with perspective, training, education, and life experience can bring to schoolchildren, but in a manner that is facilitative and managerial. We have never expected athletic coaches at schools to also play the game with their teams, yet we have for many years wanted our classroom teachers to not only coach our students but carry the ball from goal to goal, from base to base. The role that teachers, once the technology infrastructure is in place, choose to play in a classroom, may remain in flux for many years to come. But changes in that role, much of it due to the integration of technology, are afoot, and—at least in these classrooms—seem to be of benefit to both student and teacher.

These teachers are exploring teaching that is not just done to, and for, kids, but also with, and by, kids.

Not more than a couple of years back, a contestant on a public radio game show explained to the audience—after revealing she was a teacher—that she was in recent years more like, in her words, a "facilitator." This brought a huge wave of laughter from the audience, clearly chagrined at the idea of an educator being anything less, or more, than the instructor with which they were all familiar.

What these teachers talking about technology in their classrooms illustrate is that any number of roles for teachers are possible—facilitator being just one—in service to their students' learning. The probability of achievement using technology remains an open question, and will result not just from upgrading infrastructure, but also from human inputs to that infrastructure. Perhaps this underscores the other signal feature of these classrooms using technology: the expansion for everyone concerned, not just of probabilities, but just as importantly, of possibilities.

Appendix

District Data

DISTRICT DEMOGRAPHIC DATA*

Teacher	State	District	Total enrollment	White	African American	Hispanic	Asian	American Indian	Special education	Eligible for Free or Reduced Lunch	English Language Learner
Laura Bradley	CA	Petaluma City Schools	7,567	n/a	2%	27.6%	3.9%	-	13.2%	63%	13.8%
Christopher Craft	SC	District 5 of Lexington and Richland Counties	16,937	60.9%	29.8%	3.4%	3.2%	.06%	13.2%***	32.6%	3.7%
Steven Eno	CA	El Segundo Unified School District	3,415	53%	3%	22.2%	6%	0.01%	6.9%	11.7%	5.4%
Amber Kowatch	MI	Ludington Area School District	2,288	80.24%	1.57%	9.92%	1.09%	.61%	13.85%	49%	-
Jennifer Motter	PA	Forest Hills School District	1,972	97%	1%	.03%	.02%	-	14%	49%	.001%
Pernille Ripp	WI	Middleton–Cross Plains Area School District	6,622	77.6%	6.0%	8.0%	8.0%	-	10.2%	17.7%	5.5%
Josh Silver	NM	Las Cruces Public Schools**	24,668	20.1%	2.7%	74.9%	1.1%	0.4%	14.5%	64.6%	13.3%
Josh Stumpenhorst	IL	Naperville Community Unit School District 203	17,500	64.94%	6.01%	10.51%	14.84%	.17%	9.3%	13.3%	4.1%
Lindsey Taylor	NC	Gaston County Public Schools	31,284	64.7%	20%	9.5%	1.4%	.20%	12.8%	59%	4.6%

Sources: State of North Carolina, New Mexico Public Education Department, Naperville Community Unit School District 203, Forest Hills School District, California Department of Education, Middleton–Cross Plains Area School District, Ludington Area School District, South Carolina Department of Education.

*Percentages for the 2012–2013 academic year except where noted. Race and ethnicity data may not total 100 percent due to additional categories not included.

** Enrollment data for 2011–2013.

***Data for 2013–2014.

Acknowledgments

SPECIAL THANKS GOES TO Brian Foley, associate professor, Eisner College of Education, California State University, Northridge. Through Foley, I learned of the work of teachers Steven Eno and Jennifer Motter. He provided his thoughts on a number of writing projects, prior to this one, as well. I am very grateful for his help.

Dr. Richard Beach, emeritus professor of English Education, University of Minnesota, offered feedback on the initial proposal, along with ideas about how to approach aspects of educational technology that proved extraordinarily useful in formulating my questions and work with the subject teachers. Through him, I found Jessica Parker at Sonoma State University; Parker provided clarity about how technology is being scaffolded for teachers, and how, and to what extent, this is evaluated. She introduced me to teacher Laura Bradley. Barbara Treacy at Education Development Center, Inc., led me to Leslie Fetzer at NCVPS, who ultimately showed me the work of teacher Lindsey Taylor. Thank you all for your assistance.

A number of academics and education professionals provided their own insights, discussion, ideas, links, or pointers to other information sources: thanks to Christopher Harris, director, School Library System of the Genesee Valley Educational Partnership; Amy Hutchison, Iowa State University; Kerry Rice, associate Professor, Boise State University; Lisa Thumann, assistant director, School for Global Education and Innovation, Kean University; and Leigh Zeitz, associate professor, University of Northern Iowa. I greatly appreciate their time.

Teacher Joshua Stumpenhorst I found through Ronald Peck, former vice president for Technology at the National Council for Social Studies, to whom I was sent by Jordan Grote; thank you for those connections. Stumpenhorst alerted me to another amazing teacher: Pernille Ripp. Thanks to Josh for that link.

I found teachers Amber Kowatch and Joshua Silver through previous reporting I did for the *Harvard Education Letter*; Silver was recommended by his alma mater, New Mexico State University's School of Education. Teacher Christopher Craft stood out for me as a logical choice to interview because of his recognition by ISTE, and his work in middle grades STEM education.

Lisa Wolfe, of L. Wolfe Communications in Chicago, helped me locate references and archival information related to ISTE's recognition of the work of Craft and Stumpenhorst. Her persistence is appreciated.

Principals, assistant and vice principals, teacher colleagues, and administrative staff and technologists, for the schools and districts where the teachers in this book work, were incredibly giving of their time. Thanks very much for helping raise up the work of the educators profiled herein.

The staff of the Harvard Education Publishing Group, and Harvard Education Press, deserve the highest praise and thanks. My editor, Nancy Walser of the Harvard Education Press, provided an enormous range of support—from ideas about the original book proposal to journalistic advice, and from research assistance to counsel about long-form writing. Her colleagues, including the editorial board, were equally helpful in their support for the project.

In a world where everything is published—literally, if you want to auto-publish a prescheduled blog post, for instance—yesterday, the Harvard staff works carefully, and methodically.

I am grateful to the teachers in this book for providing so much information about, and perspective on, their practices and educational technology. Their work is inspiring to students and educators alike—including me.

About the Author

DAVE SALTMAN is a journalist, teacher, and tutor. In his early newspaper career, he worked for the *Washington Post*, the *Sarasota Herald-Tribune*, and States News Service; later, he worked as an online producer for America Online, and subsequently as a writer, producer, and editor for a number of Web sites. He received his BA from Clark University, an MBA from Marymount University, and a teaching credential, in English and social science, from California State University, Northridge, where he attended the Accelerated Collaborative Teacher Preparation Program (ACT), offered by the Eisner College of Education. He has volunteered as a tutor for a state-funded, free, library-based literacy program for adults and youth, in both Burbank, California, and Sonoma County, California, where he now lives. He was born in a New York City suburb, and raised outside Washington, DC, in Maryland, where he graduated high school.

He dedicates this book to his many teachers and professors, including Mrs. Keller, of Washington Avenue School, Hartsdale, New York, and Wren Abramo, Regis Boyle, and Ashby Bryson, who worked for Montgomery County (Maryland) Public Schools. They, and many others, encouraged learning, inspired achievement, and offered engagement with the world around students, and beyond school walls.

Index